D0630263

Biscuits
and
Cookies

Hamlyn Cookshelf Series

Biscuits
— and —
Cookies

Nicola Diggins

HAMLYN

The following titles are also available in this series:

Cooking with Yogurt · The Food Processor Cookbook
Mighty Mince Cookbook · Potato Cookery
Sweets and Candies · Chilli Cookbook

Front cover and inside photography by Chris Crofton
Line drawings by Patricia Capon

Published 1985 by Hamlyn Publishing
Bridge House, 69 London Road, Twickenham, Middlesex

Copyright © Hamlyn Publishing 1985
a division of The Hamlyn Publishing Group Ltd

ISBN 0 600 32475 3 (hardback)
ISBN 0 600 32473 7 (softback)

All rights reserved. No part of this publication may be reproduced,
stored in a retrieval system, or transmitted, in any form or by any
means, electronic, mechanical, photocopying, recording or otherwise,
without the prior permission of Hamlyn Publishing.

Set in 11 on 12pt Goudy Old Style
by Servis Filmsetting Ltd, Manchester
Printed in Yugoslavia

Cover *Clockwise, from top, outer ring:* Jam Rings, Almond Macaroons,
Hazelnut Fingers, Chocolate Viennese Fingers, Lemon and Honey
Buttons, chocolate-dipped Viennese Whirls, Iced Lemon Biscuit,
Gingernuts, Viennese Whirls, Strawberry Trumpets. *Clockwise, from the
top, inner ring:* Neapolitan Cookies, Jammy Face, Almond Jumbles

Contents

Useful Facts and Figures

Notes on metrication

In this book quantities are given in metric and Imperial measures. Exact conversion from Imperial to metric measures does not usually give very convenient working quantities and so the metric measures have been rounded off into units of 25 grams. The table below shows the recommended equivalents.

Ounces	Approx g to nearest whole figure	Recommended conversion to nearest unit of 25	Ounces	Approx g to nearest whole figure	Recommended conversion to nearest unit of 25
1	28	25	9	255	250
2	57	50	10	283	275
3	85	75	11	312	300
4	113	100	12	340	350
5	142	150	13	368	375
6	170	175	14	396	400
7	198	200	15	425	425
8	227	225	16 (1 lb)	454	450

Note: When converting quantities over 16 oz first add the appropriate figures in the centre column, then adjust to the nearest unit of 25. As a general guide, 1 kg (1000 g) equals 2.2 lb or about 2 lb 3 oz. This method of conversion gives good results in nearly all cases, although in certain pastry and cake recipes a more accurate conversion is necessary to produce a balanced recipe.

Liquid measures The millilitre has been used in this book and the following table gives a few examples.

Imperial	Approx ml to nearest whole figure	Recommended ml	Imperial	Aprox ml to nearest whole figure	Recommended ml
¼ pint	142	150 ml	1 pint	567	600 ml
½ pint	283	300 ml	1½ pints	851	900 ml
¾ pint	425	450 ml	1¾ pints	992	1000 ml (1 litre)

Spoon measures All spoon measures given in this book are level unless otherwise stated.

Can sizes At present, cans are marked with the exact (usually to the nearest whole number) metric equivalent of the Imperial weight of the contents, so we have followed this practice when giving can sizes.

Oven temperatures The table below gives recommended equivalents.

	°C	°F	Gas Mark		°C	°F	Gas Mark
Very cool	110	225	$\frac{1}{4}$	Moderately hot	190	375	5
	120	250	$\frac{1}{2}$		200	400	6
Cool	140	275	1	Hot	220	425	7
	150	300	2		230	450	8
Moderate	160	325	3	Very Hot	240	475	9
	180	350	4				

Notes for American and Australian users

In America the 8-fl oz measuring cup is used. In Australia metric measures are now used in conjunction with the standard 250-ml measuring cup. The Imperial pint, used in Britain and Australia, is 20 fl oz, while the American pint is 16 fl oz. It is important to remember that the Australian tablespoon differs from both the British and American tablespoons; the table below gives a comparison. The British standard tablespoon, which has been used throughout this book, holds 17.7 ml, the American 14.2 ml, and the Australian 20 ml. A teaspoon holds approximately 5 ml in all three countries.

British	American	Australian
1 teaspoon	1 teaspoon	1 teaspoon
1 tablespoon	1 tablespoon	1 tablespoon
2 tablespoons	3 tablespoons	2 tablespoons
$3\frac{1}{2}$ tablespoons	4 tablespoons	3 tablespoons
4 tablespoons	5 tablespoons	$3\frac{1}{2}$ tablespoons

An Imperial/American guide to solid and liquid measures

Imperial	American	Imperial	American
Solid measures		**Liquid measures**	
1 lb butter or		$\frac{1}{4}$ pint liquid	$\frac{2}{3}$ cup liquid
margarine	2 cups	$\frac{1}{2}$ pint	$1\frac{1}{4}$ cups
1 lb flour	4 cups	$\frac{3}{4}$ pint	2 cups
1 lb granulated or		1 pint	$2\frac{1}{2}$ cups
caster sugar	2 cups	$1\frac{1}{2}$ pints	$3\frac{3}{4}$ cups
1 lb icing sugar	3 cups	2 pints	5 cups
8 oz rice	1 cup		($2\frac{1}{2}$ pints)

Note: When making any of the recipes in this book, only follow one set of measures as they are not interchangeable.

Introduction

Although there is now a vast range of commercial biscuits to choose from, nothing can compare with the flavour and melt-in-the-mouth quality of a good home-made biscuit. An additional merit is that many home-made biscuits are inexpensive and you can make quite a saving by baking your own biscuit supply – notably when there are children to keep happy in the school holidays.

If you are a novice at biscuit making, try the recipes in the Traditional, Savoury and Semi-Sweet, or No-Need-to-Bake sections first, as these tend to be the simplest. The luxury and dessert biscuits take more time and patience, but even their preparation seems easy when compared with the complexity and pitfalls of cake making.

If you want to be really adventurous, try your hand at some of the novelty biscuits in the Kids' and Special Occasions chapters. These are bound to impress and are guaranteed original. No commercial biscuit is quite their match.

Finally, remember that most un-iced biscuits freeze well and take only minutes to thaw. So they are always on hand to serve to unexpected visitors or to enjoy at any time of day.

Traditional Biscuits

Here is a chapter of well-known and well-tried biscuits – old favourites like crisp Grantham Gingerbreads and deliciously sticky Flapjacks. Not only are the recipes in this section quick and easy to make, but their flavour is far superior to that of their shop-bought counterparts and in many cases the home-made biscuits are cheaper too!
As well as being the ideal chapter to turn to when you have the time to top up the family biscuit barrel, many of these ideas are especially good for fund-raising events. For example, why not try making a batch of Shrewsbury Biscuits for your next bazaar or coffee morning gathering? So many variations can be prepared from this one basic mixture that the recipe is ideal for baking in large quantities.
Whether you make the biscuits for a special purpose, or simply to cheer up your mid-morning coffee, you're sure to find that friends and family alike cannot resist the temptation to have just another biscuit!

Almond Macaroons

(Illustrated on front cover)

rice paper
100 g/4 oz ground almonds
175 g/6 oz caster sugar
2 tablespoons cornflour
2 egg whites, lightly beaten
$\frac{1}{4}$ teaspoon almond essence
halved blanched almonds to decorate

Line two baking trays with rice paper. Mix together the ground almonds, sugar and cornflour. Add the egg whites and almond essence and stir well to give a thick paste.

Spoon the mixture into a nylon piping bag fitted with a plain 1-cm/$\frac{1}{2}$-in nozzle. Pipe 16 rounds of the mixture at intervals on the prepared baking trays and place half a blanched almond in the centre of each.

Bake in a moderately hot oven (190 C, 375 F, gas 5) for 18–20 minutes, or until lightly browned. Allow the macaroons to cool on the tray for a few minutes, then tear the excess rice paper away and transfer the biscuits to a wire rack to cool completely. *Makes 16 almond macaroons*

Almond Jumbles

(Illustrated on front cover)

100 g/4 oz butter or margarine, softened
100 g/4 oz caster sugar
1 egg, lightly beaten
175 g/6 oz plain flour, sifted
50 g/2 oz ground almonds
caster sugar to sprinkle

Lightly grease two baking trays. Cream the butter or margarine with the sugar until very soft, light and fluffy. Gradually add the egg, beating continuously. Mix together the flour and ground almonds, then work these dry ingredients into the creamed mixture to give a fairly soft dough.

Divide the dough in two and form each half into a roll 1 cm/ ½ in in diameter on a lightly floured board. Cut off 7.5-cm/3-in lengths and form them into 'S' shapes on the prepared baking trays.

Bake in a moderate oven (180 C, 350 F, gas 4) for 20 minutes, or until the biscuits are lightly browned. Sprinkle the jumbles with caster sugar immediately they are removed from the oven. Leave to cool on the trays for a minute before transferring the biscuits to a wire rack to cool completely. *Makes 30 almond jumbles*

Grantham Gingerbreads

(Illustrated on page 33)

100 g/4 oz butter or margarine, softened
350 g/12 oz caster sugar
1 egg, lightly beaten
250 g/9 oz self-raising flour
1 teaspoon ground ginger

Lightly grease two baking trays. Cream the butter or margarine with the sugar until very soft and pale in colour. Gradually add the egg, beating continuously. Sift together the flour and ginger, then work these dry ingredients into the creamed mixture to make a firm dough.

Divide the dough into 40 and form each piece into a ball. Place the gingerbreads at intervals on the prepared baking trays. Bake in a slow oven (150 C, 300 F, gas 2) for 40–45 minutes or until well risen, hollow inside, and a pale straw colour. Remove the hot biscuits from the trays and transfer them to a wire rack to cool completely.

Continue cooking the biscuits in this way until all the mixture is used, cleaning and re-greasing the trays if necessary. *Makes 40 Grantham gingerbreads*

Gingernuts

(Illustrated on page 33)

200 g/7 oz plain flour
1 teaspoon bicarbonate of soda
1 teaspoon ground ginger
1 teaspoon mixed spice
1 teaspoon ground cinnamon
50 g/2 oz butter or margarine
100 g/4 oz demerara sugar
6 tablespoons golden syrup

Grease two baking trays. Sift the flour, bicarbonate of soda and spices into a bowl and make a well in the centre. Melt the butter or margarine, sugar and syrup in a saucepan over a low heat. Do not allow to boil. Pour the hot mixture into the well in the dry ingredients and mix thoroughly.

Allow the mixture to cool until stiff enough to handle, then roll it into small balls. Place the gingernuts well apart on the prepared baking trays. Bake one tray of gingernuts at a time in a moderately hot oven (190C, 375F, gas 5) for 10 minutes, or until dark golden brown. Allow the biscuits to cool on the trays for a minute before transferring them to a wire rack to cool completely.

Continue cooking batches of biscuits in this way until all the mixture is used, cleaning and re-greasing the trays if necessary.
Makes 35 gingernuts

Brandy Snaps

50 g/2 oz butter or margarine
50 g/2 oz caster sugar
50 g/2 oz golden syrup
50 g/2 oz plain flour
½ teaspoon ground ginger
300 ml/½ pint double cream

Line two baking trays with non-stick baking parchment and oil 3 wooden spoon handles. Melt the butter or margarine, sugar and syrup in a saucepan over a low heat. Do not allow to boil. Leave the mixture to cool slightly. Sift together the flour and ginger, then quickly beat into the melted mixture.

Drop teaspoonfuls of the mixture well apart on the prepared baking trays. Bake in a moderate oven (180 C, 350 F, gas 4) for 10 minutes, or until thinly spread and golden.

Allow the biscuits to cool on the trays for a few seconds, then, using a large palette knife, carefully remove the biscuits while they are still hot. Depending on the length of the spoon handles, quickly wrap 2 or 3 brandy snaps around each, and place on a wire rack to cool completely.

Continue cooking the biscuits in this way until all the mixture is used, re-lining the trays if necessary.

To finish the brandy snaps, whip the cream until stiff, spoon into a nylon piping bag fitted with a star nozzle and pipe it into the brandy snap shells.

Serve within an hour of filling, otherwise the biscuits will loose their crispness. *Makes 18 brandy snaps*

Garibaldi Biscuits

350 g/12 oz plain flour
100 g/4 oz icing sugar
175 g/6 oz butter or margarine
1 egg plus 1 egg yolk to glaze
75 g/3 oz currants

Lightly grease two baking trays. Sift the flour and icing sugar into a bowl and make a well in the centre. Cut the butter or margarine into small pieces and place in the well in the dry ingredients, together with the egg. Using your fingertips, gradually work the ingredients together to form a fairly soft dough.

Divide the dough in two, then roll each half into a rectangle measuring 36×30 cm/14×12 in. Spread the currants evenly over the surface of one sheet of dough, then, using a rolling pin to help you, carefully lay the second sheet of dough over the first. Re-roll to measure 38×38 cm/15×15 in and cut into biscuits measuring 4×6 cm/$1\frac{1}{2} \times 2\frac{1}{2}$ in. Using a palette knife, carefully transfer the biscuits to the prepared baking trays. Prick evenly with a fork, then chill for 30 minutes, or longer if you have time. Beat the egg yolk with a tablespoon of water and use to glaze the biscuits.

Bake the Garibaldis in a moderately hot oven (200 C, 400 F, gas 6) for 10–12 minutes, or until golden brown. Remove the hot biscuits from the trays and transfer them to a wire rack to cool completely. *Makes 60 Garibaldis*

Variation
Chocolate Garibaldis: break 225 g/8 oz milk chocolate into pieces and place the pieces in a bowl over a saucepan of hot water. Heat gently, stirring occasionally, until the chocolate has melted. Coat the cooled biscuits with the melted chocolate.

Lemon and Honey Buttons

(Illustrated on front cover)

100 g/4 oz butter or margarine, softened
75 g/3 oz caster sugar
2 tablespoons clear honey
1 egg, lightly beaten
350 g/12 oz plain flour
½ teaspoon ground cinnamon
pinch of salt

Filling
40 g/1½ oz butter or margarine
2 tablespoons clear honey
finely grated rind of 1 lemon
175 g/6 oz icing sugar
2 teaspoons lemon juice

Lightly grease two baking trays. Cream the butter or margarine with the sugar and honey until very soft, light and fluffy. Gradually add the egg, beating continuously. Sift together the flour, cinnamon and salt, then work these dry ingredients into the creamed mixture.

Divide the mixture into 50 and form each piece into a ball. Place the biscuits at intervals on the prepared baking trays and flatten each one slightly with the prongs of a fork.

Bake in a moderately hot oven (190 C, 375 F, gas 5) for 18–20 minutes, or until well browned. Remove the hot biscuits from the trays and transfer them to a wire rack to cool completely.

While the biscuits are cooling, prepare the lemon and honey filling. Cream the fat with the honey and lemon rind until very soft, light and fluffy. Sift the icing sugar and work half the quantity into the creamed mixture, then beat in the lemon juice and the remaining icing sugar. Sandwich the biscuits together in pairs with the filling. *Makes 25 lemon and honey buttons*

Orange Spice Biscuits

75 g/3 oz butter or margarine, softened
100 g/4 oz soft, light brown sugar
1 egg, lightly beaten
grated rind of 1 orange
200 g/7 oz self-raising flour
1 teaspoon ground cumin

Lightly grease two baking trays. Cream the butter or margarine with the sugar until very soft, light and fluffy. Gradually add the egg, beating continuously, then beat in the orange rind. Sift together the flour and cumin, then work these dry ingredients into the creamed mixture to make a fairly soft dough.

Form the dough into a roll 5 cm/2 in in diameter on a floured board. Wrap in cling film and chill for 2 hours, or longer if you have time. Unwrap the dough and cut it into 5-mm/¼-in slices. Place the slices well apart on the prepared baking trays.

Bake in a moderately hot oven (200 C, 400 F, gas 6) for 10–12 minutes, or until golden brown. Allow the biscuits to cool on the trays for a minute before transferring them to a wire rack to cool completely. *Makes 24 orange spice biscuits*

Cornish Fairings

100 g/4 oz plain flour
1 teaspoon baking powder
1 teaspoon bicarbonate of soda
1 teaspoon ground ginger
½ teaspoon ground cinnamon
50 g/2 oz butter or margarine
50 g/2 oz caster sugar
3 tablespoons golden syrup

Lightly grease two baking trays. Sift the flour, baking powder, bicarbonate of soda and spices into a bowl. Rub in the butter or margarine until the mixture resembles fine breadcrumbs. Stir in the sugar, then warm the syrup in a saucepan and stir it into the dry ingredients to give a stiff dough.

Divide the mixture into 20 and form each piece into a ball. Place the biscuits well apart on the prepared baking trays.

Bake in a moderately hot oven (200C, 400F, gas 6) for 8–10 minutes, or until the fairings are golden brown. Allow the biscuits to cool on the trays for a few minutes before transferring them to a wire rack to cool completely. *Makes 20 Cornish fairings*

Spice Rings

50 g/2 oz butter or margarine, softened
25 g/1 oz caster sugar
75 g/3 oz plain flour
$\frac{1}{2}$ teaspoon mixed spice
1 egg white, lightly beaten
50 g/2 oz nibbed almonds

Lightly grease two baking trays. Cream the butter or margarine with the sugar until very soft, light and fluffy. Sift together the flour and mixed spice, then gradually work these dry ingredients into the creamed mixture.

Knead gently, then roll out the dough on a lightly floured board to a thickness of 5 mm/$\frac{1}{4}$ in. Cut into rings, using first a 6-cm/$2\frac{1}{2}$-in fluted cutter and then a 2.5-cm/1-in fluted cutter. Re-roll the trimmings to produce as many biscuits as possible. Using a palette knife, carefully transfer the rings to the prepared baking trays and chill for 1–2 hours. Brush each biscuit with beaten egg white and sprinkle with the almonds.

Bake in a moderate oven (180C, 350F, gas 4) for 15 minutes, or until very lightly browned. Remove the hot biscuits from the trays and transfer them to a wire rack to cool completely. *Makes 12 spice rings*

St Catherine's Cakes

100 g/4 oz butter or margarine
100 g/4 oz caster sugar plus a little to sprinkle
1 egg, lightly beaten
200 g/7 oz self-raising flour
½ teaspoon mixed spice
25 g/1 oz ground almonds
25 g/1 oz currants

Lightly grease two baking trays. Cream the butter or margarine with the sugar until very soft, light and fluffy. Gradually add the egg, beating continuously. Sift the flour with the mixed spice, then work these dry ingredients into the creamed mixture, together with the ground almonds and currants to make a soft dough.

Divide the dough into 12 and form each piece into a long roll 7 mm/⅜ in thick, on a floured surface. Carefully coil each roll (imitating the shape of a Catherine Wheel firework) on the prepared baking trays.

Bake the biscuits in a moderate oven (180 C, 350 F, gas 4) for 20 minutes, or until golden brown. Sprinkle the St Catherine's cakes with caster sugar immediately they are removed from the oven. Leave to cool on the trays for a minute before transferring the biscuits to a wire rack to cool completely.
Makes 12 St Catherine's cakes

Cherry and Coconut Cookies

175 g/6 oz plain flour
$\frac{1}{2}$ teaspoon baking powder
$\frac{1}{4}$ teaspoon bicarbonate of soda
100 g/4 oz caster sugar
100 g/4 oz rolled oats
50 g/2 oz desiccated coconut
50 g/2 oz glacé cherries, quartered
150 ml/$\frac{1}{4}$ pint vegetable oil
1 egg, lightly beaten
4 tablespoons milk
$\frac{1}{2}$ teaspoon vanilla essence

Sift the flour, baking powder and bicarbonate of soda into a bowl. Stir in the sugar, oats, coconut and quartered glacé cherries. Make a well in the centre of the dry ingredients and add the oil, egg, milk and vanilla essence. Gradually beat the liquids into the dry ingredients until they are well mixed and a soft dough is formed.

Drop heaped teaspoonfuls of the mixture on to two ungreased baking trays. Space the biscuits well apart to allow room for spreading.

Bake in a moderately hot oven (200 C, 400 F, gas 6) for 8–10 mintues, or until golden. Leave the cookies to cool on the trays for a minute before transferring them to a wire rack to cool completely. Continue cooking the biscuits in this way until all the mixture is used, cleaning the trays between each batch.
Makes 36 cherry and coconut cookies

Coconut Chews

(Illustrated on page 33)

100 g/4 oz plain flour
1½ teaspoons bicarbonate of soda
50 g/2 oz butter or margarine
100 g/4 oz desiccated coconut
75 g/3 oz caster sugar
75 g/3 oz golden syrup

Lightly grease two baking trays. Sift the flour and bicarbonate of soda into a bowl. Rub in the butter or margarine until the mixture resembles fine breadcrumbs.

Stir in the coconut and sugar, then bind to a soft dough with the syrup. Divide the mixture into 25 and form each piece into a small ball the size of a walnut. Place the coconut chews at intervals on the prepared baking trays, allowing room for them to spread.

Bake in a moderate oven (180C, 350F, gas 4) for 12–15 minutes, or until golden brown. Allow the biscuits to cool on the trays for a minute before transferring them to a wire rack to cool completely. *Makes 25 coconut chews*

Apricot and Oat Shorties

100 g/4 oz butter or margarine, softened
50 g/2 oz soft, dark brown sugar
6 tablespoons clear honey
1 egg, lightly beaten
100 g/4 oz dried apricots (the type that need no pre-soaking)
100 g/4 oz self-raising flour, sifted
175 g/6 oz rolled oats
50 g/2 oz chopped mixed nuts

Lightly grease two baking trays. Cream the butter or margarine with the sugar and honey until very soft, light and fluffy.

Gradually add the egg, beating continuously. Chop the apricots finely and work these into the creamed mixture, together with the flour, oats and chopped nuts.

Divide the mixture into 30 and form each piece into a ball. Place the shorties at intervals on the prepared baking trays and flatten each one slightly with the blade of a knife.

Bake in a moderate oven (180C, 350F, gas 4) for 25 minutes, or until golden brown. Remove the hot biscuits from the trays and transfer them to a wire rack to cool completely. *Makes 30 apricot and oat shorties*

Malted Oaties

175 g/6 oz self-raising flour
50 g/2 oz medium oatmeal
· 50 g/2 oz malted food drink
75 g/3 oz butter or margarine
100 g/4 oz soft, light brown sugar
2 tablespoons golden syrup

Lightly grease two baking trays. Sift the flour into a bowl, stir in the oatmeal and malted food drink and make a well in the centre. Melt the butter or margarine, sugar and syrup in a saucepan over a low heat, but do not allow to boil. Pour the melted mixture into the well in the dry ingredients and mix thoroughly. While still warm, divide and quickly roll the mixture into small balls, the size of a walnut.

Place the oaties at intervals on the prepared baking trays, allowing room for them to spread. Bake in a moderately hot oven (190C, 375F, gas 5) for 12–15 minutes, or until the oaties are golden brown. Allow the biscuits to cool on the trays for a minute before transferring them to a wire rack to cool completely. *Makes 25 malted oaties*

Flapjacks

100 g/4 oz butter or margarine
100 g/4 oz soft, light brown sugar
50 g/2 oz golden syrup
225 g/8 oz rolled oats

Lightly grease a 23 × 15-cm/9 × 6-in shallow tin. Melt the butter or margarine, sugar and syrup in a saucepan over a low heat. Do not allow to boil. Remove from the heat and stir in the rolled oats. Press the mixture into the prepared tin and smooth the surface with the back of a warm metal spoon.

Bake in a moderate oven (180 C, 350 F, gas 4) for 40 minutes, or until golden brown. Mark and cut the hot mixture into fingers and leave to cool completely before removing the fingers from the tin with a palette knife. *Makes 16 flapjacks*

Variations
Date and orange flapjacks: stir 75 g/3 oz stoned and chopped dates and the grated rind of one orange into the mixture before baking.
Ginger fudge flapjacks: mix 1 teaspoon ground ginger with the oats before stirring into the melted ingredients. Bake, cut the hot mixture into fingers, cool and remove from the tin as above, then ice each flapjack with ginger fudge icing (page 125).

Pecan and Praline Cookies

100 g/4 oz butter or margarine
100 g/4 oz soft, light brown sugar
175 g/6 oz plain flour
$\frac{1}{2}$ teaspoon bicarbonate of soda
$\frac{1}{2}$ teaspoon cream of tartar
14 pecan nut halves

Filling
1 quantity Vanilla Butter Icing (page 124)
50 g/2 oz nut brittle

Lightly grease two baking trays. Cream the fat with the sugar until very soft, light and fluffy. Sift together the flour, bicarbonate of soda and cream of tartar, then work these dry ingredients into the creamed mixture to make a soft dough.

Divide the dough into 28 and form each piece into a ball. Place at intervals on the prepared baking trays and press a pecan nut in the centre of half the quantity of biscuits.

Bake in a moderate oven (180 C, 350 F, gas 4) for 20 minutes, or until lightly browned. Remove the hot biscuits from the trays and transfer them to a wire rack to cool completely.

While the biscuits are cooling, make the butter icing according to the recipe instructions. Finely crush the nut brittle with a rolling pin, add it to the butter icing and beat well. Sandwich the biscuits together in pairs with the filling. *Makes 14 pecan and praline cookies*

Coffee and Walnut Sandwiches

75 g/3 oz butter or margarine
225 g/8 oz plain flour, sifted
75 g/3 oz caster sugar
75 g/3 oz ground walnuts
1 egg, lightly beaten

Filling and decoration
1 quantity Coffee Butter Icing (page 124)
$\frac{1}{2}$ quantity Coffee Glacé Icing (page 125)
16 walnut halves to decorate

Lightly grease two baking trays. Rub the butter or margarine into the flour until the mixture resembles fine breadcrumbs. Stir in the sugar and ground walnuts, then add the egg and mix well to make a firm dough.

Knead gently, then roll out the dough on a lightly floured board to a thickness of 5 mm/$\frac{1}{4}$ in. Cut into rounds with a 5-cm/2-in plain cutter and re-roll the trimmings to produce as many biscuits as possible. Using a palette knife, carefully transfer the biscuits to the prepared baking trays. Chill for 30 minutes, or longer if you have time.

Bake in a moderately hot oven (190C, 375F, gas 5) for 15 minutes, or until very lightly browned. Remove the hot biscuits from the trays and transfer them to a wire rack to cool completely.

While the biscuits are cooling, make the butter and glacé icings according to the recipe instructions. Sandwich the biscuits together in pairs with the coffee butter icing and ice the tops of the biscuits with coffee glacé icing. To decorate, press a halved walnut in the centre of each biscuit and leave to set.
Makes 16 coffee and walnut sandwiches

Chocolate Bourbons

(Illustrated on page 33)

175 g/6 oz plain flour
25 g/1 oz cocoa
75 g/3 oz butter or margarine
50 g/2 oz caster sugar
2 tablespoons golden syrup
1 egg, beaten
granulated sugar for sprinkling

Filling
1 quantity Chocolate Butter Icing (page 124)

Lightly grease two baking trays. Sift the flour and cocoa into a bowl. Rub in the butter or margarine until the mixture resembles fine breadcrumbs. Stir in the sugar, then bind the mixture with the golden syrup and enough beaten egg to give a firm dough.

Knead lightly, then roll out the dough on a floured board to a rectangle measuring about 30 × 40 cm/12 × 16 in. Trim the edges and cut the rectangle into 32 biscuits measuring 2.5 × 7.5 cm/1 × 3 in. Using a palette knife, carefully transfer the biscuits to the prepared baking trays. Chill for 1 hour, or longer if you have time.

Bake in a moderate oven (180 C, 350 F, gas 4) for 10–15 minutes, or until darkened in colour and cooked. Sprinkle the biscuits with sugar immediately they are removed from the oven. Leave to cool on the trays for a minute before transferring them to a wire rack to cool completely.

While the biscuits are cooling, make the filling according to the recipe instructions. Sandwich the biscuits together in pairs with the chocolate butter icing. *Makes 16 chocolate Bourbons*

Custard Creams

175 g/6 oz butter or margarine
175 g/6 oz caster sugar
1 egg
350 g/12 oz plain flour
4 tablespoons custard powder

Filling
2 tablespoons custard powder
100 g/4 oz caster sugar
200 ml/7 fl oz milk
100 g/4 oz butter

Lightly grease two baking trays. Cream the butter or margarine with the sugar until very soft, light and fluffy. Add the egg yolks one at a time, beating well after each addition. Sift together the flour and custard powder, then work these dry ingredients into the creamed mixture to make a dough.

Divide the dough in two, knead lightly, then roll each half into a rectangle measuring about 30 × 15 cm/12 × 6 in on a floured board. Trim the edges, then cut each sheet of dough into smaller rectangles, measuring 5 × 4 cm/2 × 1½ in. Using a palette knife, carefully transfer the biscuits to the prepared baking trays. Prick evenly with a fork, then chill for 30 minutes, or longer if you have time.

Bake in a moderately hot oven (180C, 350F, gas 4) for 15 minutes, or until very lightly browned. Remove the hot biscuits from the trays and transfer them to a wire rack to cool completely.

While the biscuits are cooling, prepare the custard filling. Blend the custard powder and sugar with 4 tablespoons of the milk. Heat the remaining milk in a saucepan to just below boiling point. Whisk the milk into the custard mixture, then return to the pan and bring to the boil, stirring continuously. Cover the surface of the custard with wet greaseproof paper and leave on one side to cool.

Meanwhile, cream the butter until soft and fluffy, then gradually beat in the cold custard to give a soft buttercream texture. Sandwich the biscuits together in pairs with the filling. *Makes 24 custard creams*

Streusel Slices

1 quantity Shortbread Dough (page 35)
175 g/6 oz plain flour
75 g/3 oz butter or margarine
50 g/2 oz caster sugar
225 g/8 oz raspberry jam

Lightly grease a 23 × 15-cm/9 × 6-in shallow tin and make up the shortbread dough according to the recipe instructions. Press the shortbread dough into the prepared tin and smooth the surface with the back of a warm metal spoon.

Sift the flour into a bowl. Rub in the butter or margarine until the mixture resembles fine breadcrumbs, then stir in the sugar. Spread the shortbread base evenly with jam, then sprinkle the crumble over the top.

Bake the biscuit in a moderate oven (170 C, 325 F, gas 3) for 1 hour, or until it is lightly browned. Allow to cool completely in the tin before marking and cutting into fingers. *Makes 16 streusel slices*

Variation
Mincemeat streusel: substitute 225 g/8 oz mincemeat for the raspberry jam.

Shrewsbury Biscuits

100 g/4 oz butter or margarine, softened
100 g/4 oz caster sugar
grated rind of 1 lemon
1 egg, lightly beaten
350 g/12 oz plain flour, sifted

Lightly grease two baking trays. Cream the butter or margarine with the sugar and lemon rind until light and fluffy. Gradually add the egg, beating continuously, then work in the flour with the back of a wooden spoon. Knead the mixture gently, then roll it out on a lightly floured board to a thickness of 5 mm/$\frac{1}{4}$ in.

Cut the dough into rounds with a 6.5-cm/2$\frac{1}{2}$-in fluted cutter. Using a palette knife, carefully transfer the rounds to the prepared baking trays. Space the biscuits a little apart to allow room for spreading. Chill for 30 mintues, or longer if you have time.

Bake in a moderate oven (180 C, 350 F, gas 4) for 20 minutes or until lightly browned. Remove the hot biscuits from the trays and transfer them to a wire rack to cool completely. *Makes 24 Shrewsbury biscuits*

Variations
Jam rings: (*illustrated on front cover*) cut the centre from half the uncooked biscuit rounds, using small, fancy cocktail cutters. After baking and cooling as above, dust the ring biscuits with icing sugar; spread the round biscuits with redcurrant jelly and put a ring biscuit on the top of each.
Iced lemon biscuits: (*illustrated on front cover*) cut the biscuit dough into rounds with a 6.5-cm/2$\frac{1}{2}$-in plain cutter. Bake as Shrewsbury biscuits. While the biscuits are cooling, make up one quantity of glacé icing according to the recipe instructions on page 125, substituting lemon juice for the water. Add a little green food colouring to colour the icing pale green, then coat each biscuit with a little of the icing. Sprinkle with a few chopped pistachio nuts before the icing sets.

Fruit biscuits: add 50 g/2 oz dried fruit to the creamed mixture with the flour.

Chocolate biscuits: replace 25 g/1 oz of flour with 25 g/1 oz cocoa.

Orange and walnut biscuits: replace the lemon rind with the grated rind of 1 orange. Add 50 g/2 oz finely chopped walnuts to the creamed mixture with the flour.

Vanilla Sugar Biscuits

175 g/6 oz butter
350 g/12 oz plain flour, sifted
100 g/4 oz vanilla sugar
1 egg, lightly beaten
vanilla sugar for sprinkling

Lightly grease two baking trays. Rub the butter into the flour until the mixture resembles fine breadcrumbs. Stir in the vanilla sugar, then add the egg and mix well to make a fairly stiff dough.

Knead lightly, then roll out the dough on a floured board to a thickness of 5 mm/$\frac{1}{4}$ in. Cut into rounds with a 6.5-cm/2$\frac{1}{2}$-in fluted cutter and, using a palette knife, carefully transfer the biscuits to the prepared baking trays. Chill for 30 minutes, or longer if you have time.

Bake in a moderate oven (180C, 350F, gas 4) for 18–20 minutes, or until lightly browned. Sprinkle the biscuits with vanilla sugar immediately they are removed from the oven. Leave the biscuits to cool on the trays for a minute before transferring them to a wire rack to cool completely. *Makes 30 vanilla sugar biscuits*

Raisin Drops

100 g/4 oz butter or margarine, softened
50 g/2 oz caster sugar
50 g/2 oz soft, light brown sugar
1 egg, lightly beaten
$\frac{1}{2}$ teaspoon vanilla essence
100 g/4 oz plain flour
$\frac{1}{2}$ teaspoon bicarbonate of soda
75 g/3 oz raisins
50 g/2 oz chopped mixed nuts

Lightly grease two baking trays. Cream the butter or margarine with the sugars until very soft, light and fluffy. Gradually add the egg, beating continuously, then beat in the vanilla essence. Sift together the flour and the bicarbonate of soda, then work these dry ingredients into the creamed mixture, together with the raisins and nuts.

Drop heaped teaspoonfuls of the mixture on to the prepared baking tray. Space the biscuits well apart to allow room for spreading.

Bake in a moderate oven (180 C, 350 F, gas 4) for 15 minutes, or until golden. Leave the raisin drops to cool on the trays for a minute before transferring them to a wire rack to cool completely.

Continue cooking the biscuits in this way until all the mixture is used, cleaning and re-greasing the trays if necessary.
Makes 20 raisin drops

Marmalade Crunch

225 g/8 oz butter or margarine, softened
75 g/3 oz soft, light brown sugar
225 g/8 oz plain flour
25 g/1 oz rice flour
50 g/2 oz Seville orange marmalade
4 tablespoons golden syrup
75 g/3 oz cornflakes

Lightly grease and base line a 20-cm/8-in sandwich tin. Cream 175 g/6 oz butter or margarine with the sugar until very soft, light and fluffy. Sift together the flour and rice flour, then gradually work these dry ingredients into the creamed mixture to make a soft dough.

Press the dough into the prepared tin and smooth the surface with the back of a warm metal spoon. Chill for 1 to 2 hours.

Meanwhile, melt the remaining fat, together with the marmalade and syrup, in a saucepan over a low heat. Allow to cool slightly, then stir in the cornflakes. Spread this mixture evenly over the surface of the shortbread.

Bake in a moderate oven (170 C, 325 F, gas 3) for 50 minutes, or until darkened in colour and cooked. Mark and cut the hot marmalade crunch into 8 portions and leave to cool completely before removing from the tin with a palette knife. *Makes 8 pieces of marmalade crunch*

Melting Moments

(Illustrated on page 33)

100 g/4 oz butter or margarine, softened
100 g/4 oz caster sugar
1 egg, lightly beaten
175 g/6 oz self-raising flour
pinch of salt
50 g/2 oz cornflakes, crushed
halved glacé cherries to decorate

Lightly grease two baking trays. Cream the butter or margarine with the sugar until very soft, light and fluffy. Gradually add the egg, beating continuously. Sift together the flour and salt, then work these dry ingredients into the creamed mixture to make a soft dough.

Divide the dough into 30, form each piece into a ball and roll in the crushed cornflakes. Place the biscuits on the prepared baking trays, allowing room for them to spread. To decorate, press half a glacé cherry in the centre of each.

Bake the biscuits in a moderate oven (180 C, 350 F, gas 4) for 20 minutes or until golden brown. Remove the hot biscuits from the trays and transfer them to a wire rack to cool completely. *Makes 30 melting moments*

Variations

Ginger melting moments: sift 1 teaspoon ground ginger with the flour and salt before mixing into the other ingredients. Substitute small pieces of candied stem ginger for the halved glacé cherries.
Oated melting moments: substitute 50 g/2 oz rolled oats for the crushed cornflakes.

Opposite *From the top:* Gingernuts (part 12); Coconut Chews (page 20);
Melting Moments (page 32); Grantham Gingerbreads (page 11);
Chocolate Bourbons (page 25)

Marmalade Crunch

225 g/8 oz butter or margarine, softened
75 g/3 oz soft, light brown sugar
225 g/8 oz plain flour
25 g/1 oz rice flour
50 g/2 oz Seville orange marmalade
4 tablespoons golden syrup
75 g/3 oz cornflakes

Lightly grease and base line a 20-cm/8-in sandwich tin. Cream 175 g/6 oz butter or margarine with the sugar until very soft, light and fluffy. Sift together the flour and rice flour, then gradually work these dry ingredients into the creamed mixture to make a soft dough.

Press the dough into the prepared tin and smooth the surface with the back of a warm metal spoon. Chill for 1 to 2 hours.

Meanwhile, melt the remaining fat, together with the marmalade and syrup, in a saucepan over a low heat. Allow to cool slightly, then stir in the cornflakes. Spread this mixture evenly over the surface of the shortbread.

Bake in a moderate oven (170 C, 325 F, gas 3) for 50 minutes, or until darkened in colour and cooked. Mark and cut the hot marmalade crunch into 8 portions and leave to cool completely before removing from the tin with a palette knife. *Makes 8 pieces of marmalade crunch*

Melting Moments

(Illustrated on page 33)

100 g/4 oz butter or margarine, softened
100 g/4 oz caster sugar
1 egg, lightly beaten
175 g/6 oz self-raising flour
pinch of salt
50 g/2 oz cornflakes, crushed
halved glacé cherries to decorate

Lightly grease two baking trays. Cream the butter or margarine with the sugar until very soft, light and fluffy. Gradually add the egg, beating continuously. Sift together the flour and salt, then work these dry ingredients into the creamed mixture to make a soft dough.

Divide the dough into 30, form each piece into a ball and roll in the crushed cornflakes. Place the biscuits on the prepared baking trays, allowing room for them to spread. To decorate, press half a glacé cherry in the centre of each.

Bake the biscuits in a moderate oven (180 C, 350 F, gas 4) for 20 minutes or until golden brown. Remove the hot biscuits from the trays and transfer them to a wire rack to cool completely. *Makes 30 melting moments*

Variations
Ginger melting moments: sift 1 teaspoon ground ginger with the flour and salt before mixing into the other ingredients. Substitute small pieces of candied stem ginger for the halved glacé cherries.
Oated melting moments: substitute 50 g/2 oz rolled oats for the crushed cornflakes.

Opposite *From the top:* Gingernuts (part 12); Coconut Chews (page 20); Melting Moments (page 32); Grantham Gingerbreads (page 11); Chocolate Bourbons (page 25)

Petticoat Tails

175 g/6 oz butter, softened
75 g/3 oz caster sugar
225 g/8 oz plain flour
25 g/1 oz cornflour
pinch of salt
caster sugar to sprinkle

Grease a 20-cm/8-in fluted flan ring placed on a baking tray or a loose-bottom flan tin. Cream the butter with the sugar until very soft, light and fluffy.

Sift together the flour, cornflour and salt, then gradually work these dry ingredients into the creamed mixture. Press into the prepared ring or tin and smooth the surface with the back of a warm metal spoon. Prick all over with a fork and mark the round into eight equal portions. Chill for 1–2 hours.

Bake the shortbread in a moderate oven (160 C, 325 F, gas 3) for 50 minutes, or until it is a pale straw colour. Cut through between the portions while hot and sprinkle the caster sugar evenly over the top. Leave to cool in the ring or tin for a few minutes before transferring the biscuits to a wire rack to cool completely. *Makes 8 petticoat tails*

Variation
Hazelnut fingers: press the shortbread mixture into a shallow 20-cm/8-in square cake tin and cover with 175 g/6 oz sliced or roughly chopped hazelnuts.

Opposite *From the top:* Rich Chocolate Sandwich Biscuits (page 46); Florentines (page 39); Jap Cakes (page 38); Honey and Almond Shortbread (page 42)

Luxury Biscuits

As the chapter title suggests, this collection of recipes calls for highest quality ingredients. Where chocolate is called for, always choose dessert chocolate, rather than the substitute of chocolate-flavoured cake covering and when butter is listed among the ingredients, never settle for margarine.

There is no doubt that the rich, distinctive flavour of these biscuits justifies the expense involved in buying none but the best ingredients. Why not reserve this collection of sumptuous, creamy confections for those occasions when you want to indulge yourself and your friends or family in a special treat?

Apricot and Date Rolls

275 g/10 oz plain flour
150 g/5 oz butter
75 g/3 oz caster sugar, plus a little to sprinkle
grated rind of 1 lemon, plus 1 tablespoon
lemon juice
1 egg, lightly beaten
100 g/4 oz dried apricots
50 g/2 oz dried, stoneless dates
300 ml/½ pint water
50 g/2 oz demerara sugar

Lightly grease two baking trays. Sift the flour into a bowl. Rub in the butter until the mixture resembles fine breadcrumbs. Stir in the caster sugar and lemon rind, then bind the mixture to a soft dough with the egg. Knead lightly, then wrap the dough in cling film and chill for 30 minutes, or longer if you have time.

Meanwhile, make the filling. Finely chop the apricots and dates. Place them in a heavy-based saucepan with the lemon juice, water and demerara sugar. Simmer over a low heat for about 30 minutes, or until the fruit is soft and the liquid evaporated.

Roll out the dough on a lightly floured board into a rectangle measuring 15 × 40 cm/6 × 16 in, then cut it into two 7.5-cm/3-in strips. Spoon the fruit mixture down the length of each strip, 1 cm/½ in. in from one long edge. Gently roll the dough over the fruit mixture to form a long sausage shape with the join running underneath. Slice the roll into 5-cm/2-in lengths and place these at intervals on the prepared baking trays.

Bake in a moderately hot oven (200 C, 400 F, gas 6) for about 15 minutes, or until the apricot and date rolls are lightly browned. Immediately they are removed from the oven, sprinkle the biscuits with caster sugar. Allow them to cool on the trays for a few minutes before transferring the rolls to a wire rack to cool completely. *Makes 16 apricot and date rolls*

Jap Cakes

(Illustrated on page 34)

3 egg whites
225 g/8 oz caster sugar
225 g/8 oz ground almonds
a few drops of almond essence
175 g/6 oz apricot jam
$\frac{1}{2}$ quantity Glacé Icing (page 125)
pink food colouring

Line a shallow 23-cm/9-in square cake tin with non-stick baking parchment. Whisk the egg whites until stiff but not dry. Whisk in half the sugar, then fold in the remainder, together with the ground almonds and almond essence. Spread the mixture evenly in the prepared tin.

Bake in a cool oven (150 C, 300 F, gas 2) for about 30 minutes. Remove the biscuit from the oven and mark it into rounds, using a plain 6.5-cm/2$\frac{1}{2}$-in round cutter. Return to the oven and bake for a further 30 minutes, or until the biscuit is golden brown. Cool in the tin for a few minutes, then carefully transfer the rounds to a wire rack to cool completely.

While the jap cakes are cooling, rub the trimmings through a sieve, then warm the apricot jam gently in a small saucepan and sieve it into a bowl. When they are cold, brush the jap cakes evenly with the jam and roll them in the biscuit crumbs. Colour the glacé icing pale pink and place a small drop of icing in the centre of each biscuit. *Makes 9 jap cakes*

Florentines

(Illustrated on page 34)

75 g/3 oz butter
75 g/3 oz caster sugar
4 tablespoons golden syrup
75 g/3 oz nibbed almonds
75 g/3 oz glacé cherries, chopped
50 g/2 oz mixed peel
50 g/2 oz sultanas
grated rind of 2 lemons
50 g/2 oz plain flour, sifted

Decoration
350 g/12 oz plain chocolate

Line two baking trays with non-stick baking parchment. Melt the butter, sugar and syrup in a saucepan over a low heat. Do not allow the mixture to boil. Cool slightly, then stir in the remaining ingredients and mix well.

Drop teaspoonfuls of the mixture well apart on the prepared baking trays. Bake the Florentines in a moderate oven (180 C, 350 F, gas 4) for about 10 minutes, or until well spread and golden brown. Allow the biscuits to cool on the trays for a few seconds then, using a large palette knife, carefully transfer the biscuits to a wire rack to cool completely.

Meanwhile, break the chocolate into pieces and place in a bowl over a saucepan of hot water. Heat gently, stirring occasionally, until melted. Spread the bottom of each Florentine with melted chocolate and mark wavy lines on the chocolate with a fork. Allow the chocolate to set completely before serving the Florentines. *Makes 15 Florentines*

Rosewater Crescents

225 g/8 oz butter
40 g/1½ oz icing sugar
1 egg yolk
1 tablespoon milk
350 g/12 oz plain flour
1 teaspoon baking powder
50 g/2 oz toasted almonds, finely chopped
3 tablespoons rosewater
icing sugar to dust

Lightly grease three baking trays. Cream the butter with the icing sugar until very soft, light and fluffy. Beat in the egg yolk and milk. Sift together the flour and baking powder, then gradually work these dry ingredients into the creamed mixture, together with the chopped almonds.

Divide the dough into 40, and form each piece into an 8-cm/ 3½-in long roll, tapering off at each end. Arrange each roll in the form of a cresent on the baking trays. Bake the crescents in a moderate oven (180 C, 350 F, gas 4) for 15–20 minutes, or until lightly browned.

Immediately they are removed from the oven, brush the crescents with rosewater and sprinkle them with icing sugar. Remove the hot biscuits from the trays and transfer them to a wire rack to cool completely. *Makes 40 rosewater crescents*

Variation
Brandy crescents: make up the dough as for rosewater crescents, replacing the milk with 1 tablespoon brandy. When they are removed from the oven, brush the crescents with brandy instead of rosewater, otherwise follow the method for making rosewater crescents.

Pineapple Thins

50 g/2 oz butter, softened
50 g/2 oz caster sugar
50 g/2 oz candied pineapple
grated rind of 1 orange
40 g/1½ oz plain flour, sifted

Line two baking trays with non-stick baking parchment. Cream the butter with the caster sugar until very soft, light and fluffy. Finely chop the candied pineapple and stir it into the creamed mixture, together with the orange rind. Lastly, fold in the flour.

Drop heaped teaspoonfuls of the mixture onto the prepared baking trays, spacing well apart to allow room for them to spread. Flatten slightly with the back of a wet fork.

Bake the pineapple thins in a moderate oven (180 C, 350 F, gas 4) for about 8 minutes, or until they are golden brown. Using a large palette knife, carefully remove the hot biscuits from the trays and transfer them to a wire rack to cool completely. *Makes 12 pineapple thins*

Honey and Almond Shortbread

(Illustrated on page 34)

225 g/8 oz plain flour
225 g/8 oz butter
100 g/4 oz ground almonds
75 g/3 oz caster sugar
2 egg yolks
175 g/6 oz clear honey
225 g/8 oz flaked almonds

Lightly grease and base line an 18 × 23-cm/7 × 9-in Swiss roll tin. Sift the flour into a bowl. Rub in 175 g/6 oz of the butter until the mixture resembles fine breadcrumbs. Stir in the almonds, sugar and egg yolks and mix well to form a firm dough. Press the mixture into the prepared tin and smooth the surface with the back of a warm metal spoon. Chill the dough in the fridge while making the topping.

Melt the remaining butter with the honey in a large frying pan. Add the flaked almonds and cook over a gentle heat for 3–4 minutes, until the almonds are evenly coated with syrup, but do not allow the mixture to colour. Spread this mixture quickly over the dough base.

Bake the honey and almond shortbread in a moderate oven (170 C, 325 F, gas 3) for about 45 minutes, or until golden brown. Leave the shortbread in the tin to cool completely before cutting it into squares. *Makes 9 honey and almond shortbreads*

Honey and Hazelnut Creams

65 g/2½ oz plain flour
25 g/1 oz icing sugar
25 g/1 oz butter, softened
1 egg yolk

Filling
75 g/3 oz butter
75 g/3 oz clear honey
75 g/3 oz toasted hazelnuts, finely chopped, plus 6
whole roasted hazelnuts to decorate

Lightly grease six individual fluted tartlet tins and place them on a baking tray. Sift the flour into a bowl. Make a well in the centre and add the sugar, butter and egg yolk. Using your fingertips, blend the butter and egg yolk into the dry ingredients. Knead lightly to form a dough.

Wrap the dough in cling film and chill it for 30 minutes, or longer if you have time. Roll out the dough on a lightly floured board. Line the tartlet tins with the dough, re-rolling the trimmings, if necessary, to line all six. Place a piece of greaseproof paper over each biscuit case and sprinkle a few dried peas or beans on top. Alternatively, place aluminium cooking foil over each biscuit case, shiny side upwards. If you follow the latter method there is no need to use baking beans.

Bake the biscuit cases in a moderately hot oven (190 C, 375 F, gas 5) for 10 minutes, then remove the foil or greaseproof paper and beans and continue baking the tartlets for a further 12 minutes. Allow them to cool in their tins for a few minutes before transferring the biscuit cases to a wire rack to cool completely.

While the biscuits are cooling, make the filling. Cream the butter with the honey until very soft, light and fluffy. Stir in the chopped hazelnuts. Spoon the filling into the biscuit cases and decorate with hazelnuts. *Makes 6 honey and hazelnut creams*

Mocha Creams

150 g/5 oz plain flour
40 g/1½ oz caster sugar
75 g/3 oz butter, chopped
2 egg yolks

Filling and decoration
50 g/2 oz butter
3 tablespoons icing sugar
1 tablespoon milk
1 teaspoon coffee essence
50 g/2 oz plain chocolate, grated
½ quantity Coffee Glacé Icing (page 125)
18 chocolate flavoured coffee beans

Lightly grease two baking trays. Sift the flour into a bowl. Make a well in the centre and add the sugar, butter and egg yolks. Using your fingertips, blend the butter and egg yolks into the dry ingredients. Knead the mixture lightly to form a soft dough.

Wrap the dough in cling film and chill for 30 minutes, or longer if you have time. Roll the dough out on a lightly floured board to a 23-cm/9-in square. Cut it into smaller squares of 3.5 cm/1½ in. Using a palette knife, carefully transfer the biscuits to the prepared baking trays.

Bake the biscuits in a moderate oven (180 C, 350 F, gas 4) for about 18 minutes, or until golden brown. Remove the hot biscuits from the trays and transfer them to a wire rack to cool completely.

While the biscuits are cooling, make the filling. Cream the butter until very soft, light and fluffy. Make a syrup with the icing sugar and milk and beat this into the butter, together with the coffee essence and chocolate. Sandwich the biscuits together in pairs with the filling.

Make the coffee glacé icing according to the recipe instructions. Place a small dab of icing on top of each biscuit and decorate with a coffee bean. *Makes 18 mocha creams*

Chocolate Viennese Fingers

(Illustrated on front cover)

225 g/8 oz butter, softened
100 g/4 oz icing sugar, sifted
175 g/6 oz plain flour · 25 g/1 oz cornflour
25 g/1 oz cocoa · pinch of salt

Filling and decoration
1 quantity Vanilla Butter Icing (page 124)
50 g/2 oz plain chocolate, melted

Grease two baking trays and make a greaseproof paper piping bag according to the instructions on page 126.

Cream the butter with the sugar until very soft, light and fluffy. Sift together the flour, cornflour, cocoa and salt, then gradually work these dry ingredients into the creamed mixture – the resulting paste should be just soft enough to pipe. Spoon the mixture into a piping bag fitted with a large star nozzle and pipe 7.5-cm/3-in long fingers on to the prepared baking trays. Chill for 30 minutes, or longer if you have time.

Bake the fingers in a moderate oven (180 C, 350 F, gas 4) for 10–15 minutes, or until slightly darkened in colour and cooked. Remove the hot biscuits from the trays and transfer them to a wire rack to cool completely. While the biscuits are cooling, make the butter icing according to the recipe instructions, then use it to sandwich the fingers together in pairs.

To decorate the biscuits, pour the melted chocolate into the paper piping bag. Cut a tiny hole in the point of the bag and pipe a zig-zag pattern down the length of the fingers. Leave to set before serving. *Makes about 18 chocolate Viennese fingers*

Variation
Viennese whirls: omit the cocoa and increase the flour to 250 g/ 9 oz. Pipe whirls of the mixture on to the baking trays. Decorate the biscuits with glacé cherries and angelica before baking, or dip the cooled biscuits in melted chocolate.

Rich Chocolate Sandwich Biscuits

(Illustrated on page 34)

100 g/4 oz butter, softened
50 g/2 oz caster sugar
25 g/1 oz plain chocolate
100 g/4 oz self-raising flour

Filling and decoration
50 g/2 oz butter, softened
50 g/2 oz icing sugar
400 g/14 oz plain chocolate
1 tablespoon rum
50 g/2 oz milk chocolate

Lightly grease two baking trays and prepare a paper piping bag following the instructions on page 126. Cream the butter with the sugar until very soft, light and fluffy. Place the chocolate in a bowl over a saucepan of hot water. Heat gently, stirring occasionally, until melted. Stir the melted chocolate into the creamed mixture, then gradually add and fold in the flour to form a fairly firm dough.

Knead lightly, then wrap the dough in cling film and chill it for 30 minutes, or longer if you have time. Roll out the dough on a lightly floured board to a rectangle measuring 20 × 30 cm/ 8 × 12 in, then cut it into smaller rectangles, measuring 5 × 7.5 cm/2 × 3 in. Transfer the biscuits to the prepared baking trays.

Bake in a moderate oven (180 C, 350 F, gas 4) for about 18 minutes, or until slightly darkened in colour and cooked. Remove the hot biscuits from the trays and transfer them to a wire rack to cool completely.

While the biscuits are cooling, make the filling. Melt 50 g/ 2 oz of the plain chocolate as described above. Place the butter, icing sugar, melted chocolate and rum into a bowl and beat for 2–3 minutes, or until the mixture is light and fluffy. Sandwich the biscuits together in pairs with the chocolate filling and place them on a wire rack standing over a clean baking tray.

To coat the biscuits, melt the remaining plain chocolate and spoon a little over each biscuit. Smooth it over evenly to cover the surface completely. Then melt and spoon the milk chocolate into the paper piping bag and snip a small hole in the end. Pipe a zig-zag of milk chocolate down the length of each biscuit. Allow the chocolate to set before serving the biscuits. *Makes 8 rich chocolate sandwhich biscuits*

Magic Cookie Bars

225 g/8 oz plain chocolate
100 g/4 oz cornflakes
100 g/4 oz glacé cherries
50 g/2 oz flaked almonds
50 g/2 oz raisins
50 g/2 oz chopped mixed peel
1 (400-g/14.1-oz) can condensed milk

Line a 30 × 23-cm/12 × 9-in Swiss roll tin with non-stick baking parchment. Grate the chocolate and sprinkle it evenly over the base of the tin.

Place the cornflakes in a plastic bag and crush them lightly with a rolling pin. Quarter the cherries in a bowl, add the crushed cornflakes, flaked almonds, raisins and peel and mix well. Sprinkle this mixture evenly over the surface of the chocolate, then pour the condensed milk over the top.

Bake the mixture in a moderate oven (180 C, 350 F, gas 4) for about 20 minutes, or until golden brown. Mark and cut the hot mixture into squares, then leave to cool completely in the tin before removing the cookie bars with a palette knife. *Makes 15 magic cookie bars*

Rum and Nut Whirls

150 g/5 oz plain flour
50 g/2 oz butter
50 g/2 oz caster sugar
50 g/2 oz ground, roasted hazelnuts
1 egg, lightly beaten
4 tablespoons rum

Decoration
100 g/4 oz icing sugar
25 g/1 oz roasted hazelnuts, chopped

Lightly grease two baking trays. Sift the flour into a bowl. Rub in the butter until the mixture resembles fine breadcrumbs, then stir in the caster sugar and ground hazelnuts. Add the egg and half the rum and mix well to make a soft dough. Spoon the mixture into a large piping bag, fitted with a large star nozzle and pipe small rosettes at intervals on to the prepared baking trays.

Bake the biscuits in a moderate oven (180 C, 350 F, gas 4) for 15–20 minutes, or until lightly browned.

While the biscuits are baking, make the icing by blending the icing sugar with the remaining rum. Using a palette knife, carefully remove the hot biscuits from the trays and place them on a wire rack standing over a clean baking tray. Spoon a little icing over each biscuit while still hot and sprinkle the chopped hazelnuts on top. Cool the biscuits completely before serving them. *Makes 30 rum and nut whirls*

Biscuits for Special Occasions

What better way to mark traditional annual festivals than by baking biscuits particularly appropriate to the occasion? The basic biscuits can be baked in advance and stored in an airtight tin, ready to receive the finishing touches on the special day. Children will love to paint animal and star shapes for the tree on Christmas Eve, and prepare lurid creepy crawlies for the Spiders' Webs, while you do the more intricate icing. Honey Bunnies, Orange Pumpkins, or dazzling Fire Crackers to eat around the bonfire on Firework Night, will also entrance the younger members of the family.

A gift of Lemon Valentine Hearts, flamboyantly decorated Easter Bonnets, or a box full of biscuits to hang on the Christmas tree, will come as a welcome surprise to your friends and help to make the occasion memorable. Traditional festive biscuits from abroad add spice to the selection in this chapter.

Lemon Valentine Hearts

100 g/4 oz butter or margarine, softened
100 g/4 oz icing sugar
1 egg yolk
grated rind of 1 lemon
100 g/4 oz plain flour
100 g/4 oz rice flour

Decoration
1 quantity Vanilla Butter Icing (page 124)
225 g/8 oz lemon curd

Lightly grease two baking trays and make a greaseproof paper piping bag according to the instructions on page 126. Cream the fat with the sugar until very soft, light and fluffy. Beat in the egg yolk and lemon rind. Sift together the flour and rice flour and stir, then gradually work these dry ingredients into the creamed mixture and mix well to make a firm dough.

Knead the dough lightly and roll it out on a floured board to a thickness of 5 mm/⅛ in. Cut the dough, using a 6-cm/2½-in heart-shaped cutter, then, using a large palette knife, carefully transfer the biscuits to the prepared baking trays.

Bake the biscuits in a moderate oven (180 C, 350 F, gas 4) for about 10 minutes, or until lightly browned. Remove the hot biscuits from the trays and transfer them to a wire rack to cool completely.

While the biscuits are cooling, make the butter icing according to the recipe instructions. To complete the lemon Valentine hearts, fit the paper piping bag with a small star-shaped nozzle and spoon the butter icing into the bag. Pipe a border of butter icing shells around the edge of each biscuit, then flood the centres with 1–2 teaspoonfuls of lemon curd.
Makes 30 lemon Valentine hearts

Opposite *Clockwise, from top left:* Christmas Tree Cookies (page 60); Orange Pumpkins (page 58); Spider's Web (page 64); Chocolate Nest (page 57); Easter Bonnets (page 54)

Easter Biscuits

75 g/3 oz butter or margarine, softened
100 g/4 oz caster sugar plus a little to sprinkle
1 egg yolk
175 g/6 oz self-raising flour
1 teaspoon mixed spice
15 g/$\frac{1}{2}$ oz mixed peel
50 g/2 oz currants
1 tablespoon milk

Lightly grease two baking trays. Cream the butter or margarine with the sugar until very soft, light and fluffy. Beat in the egg yolk.

Sift together the flour and spice, then gradually work these dry ingredients into the creamed mixture, together with the peel and currants and enough milk to make a firm dough. Knead the dough lightly and roll it out on a floured board to a thickness of 3 mm/$\frac{1}{8}$ in.

Cut the biscuit dough into rounds using a 7.5-cm/3-in fluted cutter. Carefully transfer the biscuits to the prepared baking trays and prick each one three or four times with a fork.

Bake in a moderate oven (180 C, 350 F, gas 4) for about 20 minutes, or until lightly browned. Immediately they are removed from the oven, sprinkle the biscuits with caster sugar.

Leave the Easter biscuits to cool on the trays for a minute before transferring them to a wire rack to cool completely.
Makes 14 Easter biscuits

Opposite *From the top:* Peppermint Slice (page 75); Truffle Slice variation (page 74); Montelimar (page 74); Chocolate Caramel Crisp (page 72); Coffee and Orange Nut Slices (page 72); Truffle Slices (page 74)

Easter Bonnets

(Illustrated on page 51)

75 g/3 oz butter or margarine
225 g/8 oz plain flour, sifted
75 g/3 oz caster sugar
1 egg, lightly beaten

Decoration
100 g/4 oz marshmallows
1 quantity Vanilla Butter Icing (page 124)
a few drops each pink and yellow food colouring
sugar flowers   fruit   dragees
small lengths of baby ribbon

Lightly grease two baking trays and make two greaseproof paper piping bags according to the instructions on page 126. Rub the butter or margarine into the flour until the mixture resembles fine breadcrumbs. Stir in the sugar, then add the egg and mix well to make a firm dough.

Knead lightly, then roll the dough out on a floured board to a thickness of 3 mm/$\frac{1}{8}$ in. Cut the dough into rounds using a 6-cm/2$\frac{1}{2}$-in fluted cutter and, using a palette knife, carefully transfer the biscuits to the prepared baking trays.

Bake in a moderate oven (180 C, 350 F, gas 4) for about 20 minutes, or until lightly browned. Remove the hot biscuits from the trays and transfer them to a wire rack to cool completely.

While the biscuits are cooling, make the butter icing according to the recipe instructions. To complete the Easter bonnets, secure a marshmallow to the centre of each biscuit with a dab of butter icing. Colour half the remaining butter icing pink and the second half yellow. Spoon one colour into each of the paper piping bags, fitted with small star nozzels. Pipe a ring of pink or yellow butter icing rosettes around each marshmallow. Attach the edible decorations and small bows made with the ribbon to imitate a fancy hat, as shown in the photograph on page 51. *Makes 18 Easter bonnets*

Honey Bunnies

450 g/1 lb plain flour
1 teaspoon baking powder
grated rind of 1 lemon
50 g/2 oz butter or margarine
100 g/4 oz caster sugar
175 g/6 oz clear or set honey
1 egg, lightly beaten

Decoration
$\frac{1}{2}$ quantity Glacé Icing (page 125)

Lightly grease two baking trays and make a greaseproof paper piping bag according to the instructions on page 126. Sift the flour and baking powder into a bowl. Stir in the lemon rind and make a well in the centre of the ingredients.

Melt the butter or margarine, sugar and honey in a saucepan over a low heat. Do not allow to boil. Cool until lukewarm, then pour the mixture into the well in the dry ingredients. Add the egg and mix well to make a firm dough.

Knead lightly, then roll the dough out on a floured board to a thickness of 3 mm/$\frac{1}{8}$ in. Cut the dough, using a rabbit-shaped cutter, or cut out a rabbit shape from cardboard, place on top of the dough and cut round it. Using a large palette knife, carefully transfer the biscuits to the prepared baking trays.

Bake the honey bunnies in a hot oven (220 C, 425 F, gas 7) for 8–10 minutes, or until darkened in colour and cooked. Leave the biscuits to cool on the trays for a minute before transferring them to a wire rack to cool completely.

While the biscuits are cooling, make the glacé icing according to the recipe instructions. To decorate the biscuits, pour the glacé icing into the paper piping bag. Cut a tiny hole in the point of the bag and pipe rabbit features, waistcoats and buttons on to each biscuit. *Makes 36 honey bunnies*

Simnel Biscuits

50 g/2 oz butter or margarine, softened
25 g/1 oz vanilla sugar or caster sugar
75 g/3 oz plain flour, sifted

Decoration
50 g/2 oz apricot jam
225 g/8 oz marzipan
$\frac{1}{2}$ quantity Glacé Icing (page 125)
50 g/2 oz sugar eggs

Lightly grease a baking tray. Cream the butter or margarine with the sugar until very soft, light and fluffy, then gradually work the flour into this creamed mixture to make a firm dough.

Knead lightly, then roll out the dough on a floured board to a thickness of 5 mm/$\frac{1}{4}$ in. Cut into 6 rounds, using a 7.5-cm/3-in cutter and carefully transfer the biscuits to the prepared baking tray. It may be necessary to knead and re-roll the trimmings to make 6 biscuits.

Bake in a moderate oven (180 C, 350 F, gas 4) for about 18–20 minutes, or until lightly browned. Remove the hot biscuits from the tray and transfer them to a wire rack to cool completely.

To decorate the biscuits, warm the jam and lightly brush each biscuit with it. Divide the marzipan into 12 and form each piece into a 25-cm/10-in long roll. Twist the strands together in pairs and form each twist into a ring around the edge of each biscuit, pressing down firmly. Place the biscuits under a hot grill for 2–3 minutes to lightly brown the marzipan, then leave them to cool completely.

While the biscuits are cooling, make the glacé icing according to the recipe instructions. To complete the biscuits, flood the centre of each one with two or three teaspoons of glacé icing and decorate with the sugar eggs. Allow the icing to set before serving the biscuits. *Makes 6 simnel biscuits*

Chocolate Nests

(Illustrated on page 51)

50 g/2 oz butter or margarine, softened
25 g/1 oz caster sugar
65 g/2½ oz plain flour
15 g/½ oz cocoa powder

Decoration
½ quantity Chocolate Butter Icing (page 124)
3 milk chocolate flake bars
30 small, foil-covered milk chocolate eggs

Lightly grease a baking tray. Cream the butter or margarine with the sugar until very soft, light and fluffy. Sift together the flour and cocoa powder, then work these dry ingredients into the creamed mixture.

Knead gently, then roll out the dough on a lightly floured board to a thickness of 5 mm/¼ in. Cut the dough into 6 rounds, using a 7.5-cm/3-in plain cutter and, using a large palette knife, carefully transfer the biscuits to the prepared baking tray. It may be necessary to knead and re-roll the trimmings to make 6 biscuits.

Bake in a moderate oven (180C, 350F, gas 4) for 18–20 minutes, or until darkened in colour and cooked. Allow the biscuits to cool on the tray for a minute before transferring them to a wire rack to cool completely.

While the biscuits are cooling, make the butter icing according to the recipe instructions. To complete the chocolate nests, spoon or pipe a circle of butter icing a fraction in from the edge of each biscuit. Cut the flakes into large pieces and stick these to the butter icing to build up the walls of the nests. Fill each nest with a few eggs before serving. *Makes 6 chocolate nests*

Orange Pumpkins
(Illustrated on page 51)

100 g/4 oz butter or margarine, softened
100 g/4 oz caster sugar
2 egg whites, lightly beaten
grated rind of 2 oranges
a few drops orange food colouring
350 g/12 oz plain flour, sifted

Decoration
$\frac{1}{2}$ quantity Glacé Icing (page 125)
a few drops green food colouring
cream baby ribbon ·

Lightly grease two baking trays, prepare and cut a pumpkin pattern, 6 cm/2$\frac{1}{2}$ in. in diameter, out of cardboard, and make two greaseproof paper piping bags according to the instructions on page 126.

Cream the butter or margarine with the sugar until very soft, light and fluffy. Gradually add the egg whites, beating continuously. Beat in the orange rind and enough food colouring to give a deep orange colour, then work in the sifted flour and mix well to make a fairly firm dough.

Knead the dough lightly, then wrap it in cling film and chill for 30 minutes, or longer if you have time. Roll the dough out on a lightly floured board, to a thickness of 5 mm/$\frac{1}{4}$ in. Make the pumpkin shapes by placing the cardboard pattern on top of the dough and cutting round it. Re-roll the trimmings to produce as many biscuits as possible. With a skewer, make a hole near the top of each biscuit, then carefully transfer the biscuits to the prepared baking trays.

Bake the orange pumpkins in a moderately hot oven (190 C, 375 F, gas 5) for 20 minutes, or until darkened in colour and cooked. Remove the hot biscuits from the trays and transfer them to a wire rack to cool completely.

While the biscuits are cooling, make the glacé icing according to the recipe instructions. To decorate the biscuits, pour half the glacé icing into one of the paper piping bags. Cut a tiny hole in the point of the bag and pipe eyes, nose and mouth in the centre of each biscuit. Colour the remaining icing bright green, pour it into the second piping bag, cut a tiny hole in the point of the bag, and pipe vertical lines over the biscuits to represent the 'ribs' of a pumpkin.

Allow the icing to set completely before threading lengths of ribbon through the holes near the tops of the biscuits. *Makes 18 orange pumpkins*

Fire Crackers

225 g/8 oz butter or margarine, softened
100 g/4 oz icing sugar, sifted
225 g/8 oz plain flour
50 g/2 oz cornflour
pinch of salt
a few drops each red, blue and green food
colouring

Lightly grease two baking trays. Cream the butter or margarine with the sugar until very soft, light and fluffy. Sift together the flour, cornflour and salt, then gradually work these dry ingredients into the creamed mixture – the resulting paste should be just soft enough to pipe.

Divide the mixture into three, then work a different food colouring into each portion. Fit a vegetable piping bag with a medium-sized star nozzle. Spoon the red dough down the left side of the bag, the blue down the centre and the green dough down the right hand side of the bag. Pipe 7.5-cm/3-in lengths of dough on to the prepared baking trays, zig-zagging the mixture from side to side to represent fire crackers. Chill the biscuits for 30 minutes, or longer if you have time.

Bake the fire crackers in a moderate oven (180 C, 350 F, gas 4) for about 15 minutes, or until darkened in colour and cooked. Remove the hot biscuits from the trays and transfer them to a wire rack to cool completely. *Makes 18 fire crackers*

Christmas Tree Cookies

(Illustrated on page 51)

450 g/1 lb plain flour
$\frac{1}{2}$ teaspoon salt
275 g/10 oz butter or margarine
225 g/8 oz icing sugar
2 eggs, lightly beaten

Decoration
3–4 egg yolks
3–4 food colourings
red baby ribbon

Lightly grease three baking trays. Sift the flour and salt into a bowl. Rub in the butter or margarine until the mixture resembles fine breadcrumbs. Stir in the icing sugar, then add the beaten eggs and mix well to make a firm dough.

Knead lightly, then roll the dough out on a floured board to a thickness of 5 mm/$\frac{1}{4}$ in. Use Christmas cutters, for example, star, Christmas tree and animal shapes, to cut the dough. With a skewer, make a hole near the top of each biscuit, then, using a large palette knife, carefully transfer the biscuits to the prepared baking trays. Chill for 30 minutes, or longer if you have time.

Partially bake the cookies in a moderate oven (180C, 350F, gas 4) for 8 minutes. Meanwhile, blend each egg yolk with a different food colouring, in sufficient quantity to give good strong colours. Using a soft artist's brush, paint the colours on the partially baked biscuits before returning them to the oven for a further 10 minutes.

Remove the hot biscuits from the trays and transfer them to a wire rack to cool completely. When the biscuits are cold, thread the ribbon through the holes and hang the cookies on the tree. *Makes about 80 Christmas cookies*

Variation
Iced Christmas tree cookies: prepare the biscuits as above, but bake for 15–20 minutes, or until lightly browned in colour and

cooked. Cool the cookies completely. While they are cooling, make 1 quantity royal icing according to the recipe instructions on page 126. Ice the cookies and decorate them with dragees.

Mincemeat Shortbread

175 g/6 oz butter or margarine, softened
75 g/3 oz caster sugar plus 1 tablespoon to
sprinkle
225 g/8 oz plain flour
25 g/1 oz rice flour
175 g/6 oz mincemeat

Lightly grease a 15 × 23-cm/6 × 9-in shallow cake tin. Cream the butter or margarine with the sugar until very soft, light and fluffy. Sift together the flour and rice flour, then gradually work these dry ingredients into the creamed mixture to make a fairly firm dough.

Press half the dough into the prepared tin and smooth the surface with the back of a warm metal spoon. Spread the mincemeat thinly over the dough, then press the remaining dough evenly over the top. Prick all over the surface with a fork and mark the rectangle into 16 fingers.

Bake the shortbread in a moderate oven (160 C, 325 F, gas 3) for about 1 hour, or until it is a pale straw colour. Cut through between the portions while hot and sprinkle the caster sugar evenly over the top of the shortbread.

Leave to cool in the tin for a few minutes before transferring the fingers to a wire rack to cool completely. *Makes 16 pieces of mincemeat shortbread*

Snowballs

175 g/6 oz butter or margarine, softened
225 g/8 oz caster sugar
2 egg yolks
350 g/12 oz plain flour
½ teaspoon bicarbonate of soda
75 g/3 oz desiccated coconut
2 tablespoons orange juice

Decoration
450 g/1 lb apricot jam
350 g/12 oz shredded coconut

Lightly grease two baking trays. Cream the butter or margarine and sugar until very soft, light and fluffy. Add the egg yolks one at a time, beating well after each addition.

Sift the flour with the bicarbonate of soda, then work these dry ingredients into the creamed mixture, together with the desiccated coconut and the orange juice. Divide the mixture into 20 and form each piece into a ball. Place the biscuits on the prepared baking trays, allowing room for them to spread.

Bake in a moderately hot oven (190 C, 375 F, gas 5) for about 20 minutes, or until golden brown. Remove the hot biscuits from the trays and transfer them to a wire rack to cool completely.

Meanwhile, gently heat the jam in a saucepan, then pass it through a sieve to give a smooth syrup. Sandwich the biscuits together in pairs with a little of the jam, then brush the remaining jam over the surface of each biscuit and roll the biscuits in shredded coconut. Allow the coating to set for a few minutes before serving the snowballs. *Makes 10 snowballs*

Spritz Cookies

350 g/12 oz butter or margarine, softened
225 g/8 oz caster sugar
1 egg, lightly beaten
1 teaspoon vanilla essence
$\frac{1}{2}$ teaspoon almond essence
575 g/1$\frac{1}{4}$ lb plain flour
1 teaspoon baking powder

Decoration
vanilla sugar
ground nutmeg

Lightly grease two baking trays. Cream the butter or margarine with the sugar until very soft, light and fluffy. Gradually add the egg, beating continuously, then beat in the flavourings. Sift together the flour and baking powder, then work these dry ingredients into the creamed mixture.

Force the mixture through a cookie press on to the prepared baking trays. Chill for 30 minutes, or longer if you have time.

Bake the biscuits in a moderately hot oven (200 C, 400 F, gas 6) for 10 minutes, or until lightly browned. Immediately they are removed from the oven, sprinkle the vanilla sugar and a little nutmeg over the cookies. Leave to cool on the trays for a minute before transferring the biscuits to a wire rack to cool completely. *Makes about 120 spritz cookies*

Spiders' Webs

(Illustrated on page 51)

175 g/6 oz plain flour
175 g/6 oz self raising flour
175 g/6 oz butter or margarine
175 g/6 oz caster sugar
1 egg, lightly beaten

Decoration
50 g/2 oz marzipan
a few drops green food colouring
double quantity Glacé Icing (page 125)
a few drops black food colouring
cream baby ribbon

Lightly grease two baking trays and make a greaseproof paper piping bag according to the instructions on page 126. Sift the plain and self-raising flours into a bowl and rub in the butter or margarine until the mixture resembles fine breadcrumbs. Stir in the sugar, then add the egg and mix well to make a fairly firm dough.

Knead the dough lightly, then roll it out on a floured board to a thickness of 3 mm/⅛ in. Cut into rounds using an 8.5-cm/3½-in plain round cutter. With a skewer make a hole near the top of each biscuit, then, using a palette knife, carefully transfer the biscuits to the prepared baking trays. Chill for 30 minutes, or longer if you have time.

Bake in a moderately hot oven (190 C, 375 F, gas 5) for 10–15 minutes, or until golden brown. Remove the hot biscuits from the trays and transfer them to a wire rack to cool completely.

While the biscuits are cooling, add enough colouring to the marzipan to produce a bright green. Divide the marzipan into 14 pieces and model each piece into a spider. Make the glacé icing according to the recipe instructions. Remove 4 tablespoons of the icing, add the black food colouring and spoon the icing into the paper piping bag. Coat each biscuit in turn with a smooth layer of the remaining white glacé icing. Cut a tiny hole in the point of the paper piping bag and pipe a spiral of black icing over the white icing before the latter sets. Dip a skewer, or the point of a knife, into cold water briefly, and draw it across the spiral, from the centre of the biscuit to the edge. Continue drawing lines at an equal distance apart until the web is complete.

To complete the biscuits, place a spider on each web, thread ribbon through the holes and hang up the spiders webs. *Makes 14 spiders webs*

Linz Tart

100 g/4 oz butter or margarine, softened
175 g/6 oz caster sugar
2 eggs, lightly beaten
225 g/8 oz plain flour
100 g/4 oz self-raising flour
100 g/4 oz ground almonds
225 g/8 oz seedless raspberry jam

Lightly grease a 30 × 20-cm/12 × 8-in Swiss roll tin. Cream the butter or margarine with the sugar until very soft, light and fluffy. Gradually add the eggs, beating continuously. Sift the flours together and stir in the ground almonds, then work these dry ingredients into the creamed mixture.

Press two thirds of the dough into the prepared tin and smooth the surface with the back of a warmed metal spoon. Spread the jam evenly over the top. Roll the remaining dough into long sausage shapes, 1 cm/$\frac{1}{2}$ in. in diameter. Place these on top of the jam in a criss-cross, lattice pattern.

Bake the tart in a moderate oven (180 C, 350 F, gas 4) for about 40 minutes, or until the lattice is lightly browned. Leave to cool in the tin. When cold, mark and cut the tart into 12 squares. *Makes 12 pieces of Linz tart*

Pretzels

100 g/4 oz butter or margarine, softened
150 g/5 oz icing sugar
2 tablespoons golden syrup
1 egg, lightly beaten
275 g/10 oz plain flour

Decoration
double quantity Glacé Icing (page 125)
2 tablespoons lemon juice
50 g/2 oz coloured coffee crystals

Lightly grease two baking trays. Cream the butter or margarine with the icing sugar and syrup until very soft, light and fluffy. Gradually add the egg, beating continuously, then work in the flour and mix well to make a soft dough.

Divide the dough into 30, then form each piece into a pencil thin roll 25 cm/10 in long. Form each roll into a pretzel shape on the baking tray. Loop the strip of dough into a loosely knotted circle, leaving fairly long ends. Press the ends neatly on the dough at the base of the circle. Chill for 30 minutes, or longer if you have time.

Bake the pretzels in a moderately hot oven (190 C, 375 F, gas 5) for 10–12 minutes, or until lightly browned. Leave to cool on the trays for a minute before transferring the biscuits to a wire rack to cool completely.

While the biscuits are cooling, make the glacé icing according to the recipe instructions. To decorate the pretzels, thin the glacé icing with the lemon juice until it just coats the back of a spoon. Quickly spoon the glaze over the pretzels and sprinkle the coffee crystals evenly over the top before the glaze sets.
Makes 30 pretzels

No-Need-to-Bake
Biscuits

Gooey, nutty and fruity confections figure in this chapter of biscuits that do not require baking. They are ideal for replenishing the biscuit barrel when you have neither the time nor inclination to turn the oven on specially to bake a tray of biscuits, but are every bit as morish as baked biscuits. The photograph on page 52 illustrates how smaller versions of the biscuits are the perfect accompaniment to morning or after-dinner coffee. Your children will probably invade the kitchen to participate in the preparation of these goodies, which is simplicity itself.

Sesame Seed Snaps

175 g/6 oz granulated sugar
150 ml/¼ pint water
100 g/4 oz golden syrup
1 teaspoon powdered glucose
25 g/1 oz butter or margarine
1 teaspoon bicarbonate of soda
100 g/4 oz sesame seeds

Line a baking tray with non-stick baking parchment. Place the sugar, water, syrup and glucose in a large, heavy-based saucepan. Heat gently, stirring occasionally, until the sugar has dissolved. Bring to the boil and boil steadily to 150 C/300 F, stirring continuously.

Remove from the heat and stir in the butter or margarine and bicarbonate of soda; at this point the mixture will foam up. Stir well, then add and stir in the sesame seeds. Working quickly, pour the mixture on to the prepared tray. Using a warm knife, spread it evenly over the surface of the tray.

Leave the mixture to set for 2–3 minutes, then mark it into 3.5 × 6-cm/1½ × 2½-in pieces. Break into pieces when completely cold. *Makes about 16 sesame seed snaps*

Granola Bars

225 g/8 oz soft, light brown sugar
100 g/4 oz butter
100 g/4 oz rolled oats
50 g/2 oz rye flakes
25 g/1 oz hazelnuts, roughly chopped
50 g/2 oz raisins

Lightly grease an 18 × 28-cm/7 × 11-in shallow tin. Place the sugar, butter, oats, rye flakes and hazelnuts in a large, heavy-based saucepan.

Heat gently, stirring occasionally, until the sugar has dissolved and the butter has melted. Increase the temperature slightly and continue to cook, stirring continuously, until the sugar caramelises and the oats turn a light golden brown.

Quickly stir in the raisins and press the mixture into the prepared tin, levelling the surface with the back of an oiled metal spoon. Mark the mixture into 12 fingers while still warm, then break it into pieces when quite cold. *Makes 12 granola bars*

Marbled Squares

100 g/4 oz plain chocolate
100 g/4 oz milk chocolate
100 g/4 oz white chocolate
100 g/4 oz butter or margarine
6 tablespoons golden syrup
125 g/4½ oz Special K

Lightly grease and base line an 18-cm/7-in square shallow cake tin. Break the plain, milk and white chocolates into pieces and place them in separate bowls. Add one third of the butter or margarine and 2 tablespoons of syrup to each bowl. Place each bowl over a saucepan of hot water and heat the chocolate and syrup gently, stirring occasionally, until melted.

Divide the cereal evenly between the bowls and fold it in thoroughly. Place alternate teaspoonfuls of the mixtures into the prepared tin to give a marbled effect. Chill the biscuit in the refrigerator until set before cutting into squares. *Makes 16 marbled squares*

Peanut Bars

300 g/10 oz peanut butter
175 g/6 oz soft, light brown sugar
8 tablespoons golden syrup
1 teaspoon vanilla essence
75 g/3 oz Rice Krispies

Lightly grease a 23-cm/9-in square shallow tin. Place the peanut butter, sugar and syrup in a bowl over a saucepan of hot water. Heat gently, stirring occasionally, until the ingredients have melted. Stir in the vanilla essence and cereal.

Press the mixture into the prepared tin and level the surface with the back of a metal spoon. Chill in the refrigerator until firm, then cut into bars. *Makes 27 peanut bars*

Toffee Nut Bubbles

100 g/4 oz butter or margarine
$\frac{1}{2}$ (400-g/14.1-oz) can condensed milk
2 tablespoons golden syrup
50 g/2 oz Brazil nuts, roughly chopped
50 g/2 oz Rice Krispies

Lightly grease a 23 × 15-cm/9 × 6-in shallow tin. Melt the fat, condensed milk and syrup in a saucepan over a low heat. Bring to the boil and boil steadily for 5 minutes, stirring continuously.

Remove from the heat and stir in the Brazil nuts and cereal. Press the mixture into the prepared tin and level the surface with the back of a metal spoon. Chill in the refrigerator until firm, then mark and cut into squares. *Makes 12 toffee nut bubbles*

Date and Banana Squares

225 g/8 oz dates
225 g/8 oz bananas
juice of 1 lemon
2 tablespoons clear honey
150 ml/$\frac{1}{4}$ pint water
225 g/8 oz soft, light brown sugar
100 g/4 oz butter
175 g/6 oz rolled oats

Lightly grease an 18-cm/7-in square shallow cake tin. Roughly chop the dates and bananas. Place them in a heavy-based saucepan, together with the lemon juice, honey and water. Simmer the mixture gently over a low heat for about 30 minutes, or until softened. Leave it on one side to cool.

Meanwhile, make the base and topping. Place the sugar, butter and oats in a large, heavy-based saucepan. Heat these ingredients gently, stirring occasionally, until the sugar has dissolved and the butter has melted. Increase the temperature slightly and continue to cook, stirring continuously, until the sugar caramelises and the oats turn a light golden brown.

Spoon half the mixture into the prepared tin and level the surface with the back of an oiled metal spoon. Spoon the date filling over the base, then top with the remaining oat mixture. Press down lightly with the spoon and mark the date and banana biscuit into squares while still warm. Leave to cool completely before cutting the biscuit into squares. *Makes 16 date and banana squares*

Coffee and Orange Nut Slices

(Illustrated on page 52)

300 ml/½ pint double cream
2 tablespoons golden syrup
1 tablespoon coffee essence
grated rind of 1 orange
100 g/4 oz butter, chilled
225 g/8 oz shortbread biscuits, finely crushed
100 g/4 oz walnuts, chopped

Pour the cream into a large, heavy-based saucepan. Gradually bring to the boil, stirring occasionally, and continue to simmer until the volume of cream has reduced by half.

Remove the cream from the heat and stir in the syrup, coffee essence and orange rind. Cut the butter into small pieces and gradually whisk it into the cream mixture, then stir in the biscuit crumbs.

Chill the mixture until it is just firm enough to handle. Form it into a roll 6.5 cm/2½ in in diameter and coat the roll with the chopped walnuts. Wrap the coffee and orange nut roll in cling film and refrigerate until firm, then cut it into 24 even slices.
Makes 24 coffee and orange nut slices

Chocolate Caramel Crisps

(Illustrated on page 52)

2 Mars bars
50 g/2 oz butter or margarine
2 tablespoons golden syrup
50 g/2 oz cornflakes

Cut the Mars bars into small pieces and place them in a bowl over a saucepan of hot water. Add the fat and syrup and heat gently, stirring occasionally, until the mixture has melted.

Stir in the cornflakes, then, using two spoons, divide the chocolate caramel crisps between 24 paper sweet cases. Chill the crisps in the refrigerator until set before serving. *Makes 24 chocolate caramel crisps*

Chocolate Refrigerator Crunch

225 g/8 oz milk chocolate
100 g/4 oz plain chocolate
100 g/4 oz butter or margarine
100 g/4 oz shortcake biscuits
50 g/2 oz marzipan, chopped
50 g/2 oz glacé cherries
50 g/2 oz sultanas
50 g/2 oz raisins
2 tablespoons brandy

Lightly grease and line a 20-cm/8-in sandwich tin. Break the milk chocolate and plain chocolate into pieces and place the pieces in a bowl, over a saucepan of hot water. Add the butter or margarine and heat gently, stirring occasionally, until the chocolate and fat have melted.

Break the biscuits into small pieces and stir them into the chocolate mixture, together with the remaining ingredients.

Press the mixture into the prepared tin and level the surface with the back of a metal spoon. Chill the chocolate crunch in the refrigerator until firm, then mark and cut the round into 12 equal pieces. *Makes 12 pieces of chocolate crunch*

Montelimar

(Illustrated on page 52)

175 g/6 oz white marshmallows
1 tablespoon lemon juice
50 g/2 oz blanched almonds
50 g/2 oz shortcake biscuits
25 g/1 oz glacé cherries
25 g/1 oz angelica
50 g/2 oz Special K

Grease and base line a 15-cm/6-in square shallow tin. Using scissors dipped in boiling water, cut the marshmallows into small pieces. Place them in a bowl over a saucepan of hot water. Add the lemon juice and heat gently, stirring occasionally, until the marshmallows have melted.

Meanwhile, prepare the remaining ingredients. Roughly chop the almonds and crumble the shortcake biscuits, quarter the glacé cherries and finely chop the angelica. Stir these ingredients into the melted marshmallows, together with the cereal.

Spoon the mixture into the prepared tin and level the surface with the back of a warmed metal spoon. Chill the montelimar until firm, then mark and cut it into 16 squares with a knife dipped in boiling water. *Makes 16 pieces of montelimar*

Truffle Slices

(Illustrated on page 52)

175 g/6 oz plain chocolate
75 g/3 oz butter
100 g/4 oz icing sugar
100 g/4 oz digestive biscuits, crushed
2 tablespoons rum
100 g/4 oz chocolate flavoured sugar strands

Break the chocolate into pieces and place the pieces in a bowl over a saucepan of hot water. Add the butter and heat gently, stirring occasionally, until the chocolate and butter have melted. Sift the icing sugar and stir it into the chocolate mixture, together with the crushed biscuits and rum.

Leave the mixture to cool until it is just firm enough to handle. Form the mixture into a roll, 5 cm/2 in in diameter, and coat it with the chocolate sugar strands. Wrap in cling film and refrigerate the truffle roll until firm, then cut it into 20 even slices. *Makes 20 truffle slices*

Peppermint Slices
(Illustrated on page 52)

150 g/5 oz butter
175 g/6 oz malted milk biscuits, finely crushed
100 g/4 oz caster sugar
4 tablespoons milk
175 g/6 oz icing sugar, sifted
1 teaspoon peppermint essence
a few drops of green food colouring
175 g/6 oz plain chocolate

Lightly grease and line a 23 × 15-cm/9 × 6-in shallow tin. Melt 75 g/3 oz of the butter and stir in the biscuit crumbs. Press into the prepared tin and level the surface with the back of a metal spoon.

Melt the remaining butter with the caster sugar and milk. Stir over a gentle heat to dissolve the sugar. Bring to the boil and boil steadily for 1 minute. Cool until just warm, then beat in the icing sugar, peppermint essence and a few drops of colouring. Pour the mixture over the biscuit base. Chill in the refrigerator until firm.

Meanwhile, break the chocolate into pieces and melt in a basin over a saucepan of hot water. Spread the chocolate thinly over the peppermint icing and allow it to set before cutting the peppermint biscuit into slices. *Makes 16 peppermint slices*

Coconut Shortbread

75 g/3 oz butter
175 g/6 oz malted milk biscuits, finely crushed
225 g/8 oz caster sugar
5 tablespoons milk
65 g/2½ oz desiccated coconut

Decoration
50 g/2 oz plain chocolate

Grease and base line a 23 × 15-cm/9 × 6-in shallow tin and make a greaseproof paper piping bag according to the instructions on page 126. Melt the butter and stir in the biscuit crumbs. Press the mixture into the prepared tin and level the surface with the back of a metal spoon. Place the biscuit base in the refrigerator while making the topping.

Dissolve the sugar in the milk over a low heat, then bring to the boil and boil gently for about 10 minutes, or until the temperature reaches 116C/240F.

Remove the pan from the heat and stir in the coconut. Pour the mixture over the biscuit base quickly, spreading it evenly. Leave until half set, then mark the coconut shortbread into 16 fingers. Cut it into pieces when quite cold.

Meanwhile, melt the chocolate in a basin over a saucepan of hot water. Pour the chocolate into the paper piping bag. Cut a tiny hole in the point of the bag and pipe a zig-zag pattern down the length of the fingers. Leave the chocolate to set before serving the shortbreads. *Makes 16 pieces of coconut shortbread*

Cookies
for Kids

The recipes in this chapter will delight your children or young visitors, and show how you can really go to town decorating biscuits with colourful icings and sweets. For instance, let your imagination run riot in creating Lollipop faces, Chocolate Monsters and Milk Mice, or in dressing up the Three Bears.

Ideal for special treats, picnics, or for brightening up the table for children's parties, an intriguing biscuit, such as a Chocolate Boat complete with sail and a cargo of brightly coloured sweets, can be given to each child to take home from a party, providing an excellent alternative to buying special gifts. To continue in practical vein, Banana and Chocolate Chip Cookies and Peanut Butter Cookies make satisfying lunch box fillers for your children to take to school.

Alphabet Biscuits

100 g/4 oz margarine or butter, softened
100 g/4 oz icing sugar
grated rind of 1 lemon
175 g/6 oz plain flour

Lightly grease three baking trays. Cream the fat with the icing sugar until very soft, light and fluffy, then beat in the lemon rind. Sift the flour into a bowl, then gradually work it into the creamed mixture – the resulting paste should be just soft enough to pipe.

Spoon the mixture into a piping bag fitted with a medium-sized star nozzle. Pipe 7.5-cm/3-in letters or numerals on to the prepared baking trays. Chill them for 30 minutes, or longer if you have time.

Bake the letters in a moderate oven (180 C, 350 F, gas 4) for 10–15 minutes, or until lightly browned. Allow the biscuits to cool on the trays for a few minutes before transferring them to a wire rack to cool completely. *Makes about 24 alphabet biscuits*

Chocolate Boats

(Illustrated on page 85)

225 g/8 oz plain flour
150 g/5 oz butter or margarine
50 g/2 oz ground almonds
100 g/4 oz caster sugar
1 egg, lightly beaten

Decoration
350 g/12 oz chocolate flavoured cake covering
1 packet each of liquorice allsorts
smarties   jelly tots   tiger tots   dolly tots
24 cocktail sticks and paper for sails

Lightly grease 24 10-cm/4-in boat-shaped pastry moulds. Sift the flour into a bowl. Rub in the butter or margarine until the mixture resembles fine breadcrumbs. Stir in the almonds, sugar and egg and mix together quickly to make a firm dough.

Knead the dough lightly, then wrap it in cling film and chill for 30 minutes, or longer if you have time. Roll out the dough on a lightly floured board to a thickness of 5 mm/$\frac{1}{4}$ in. Using a rolling pin to help you, lift the dough over the moulds. Carefully press the dough into the base and sides of each tin. Trim away any excess pastry by rolling the rolling pin over the top of the moulds. Prick the base of each boat all over with a fork and line each one with greaseproof paper and baking beans, or aluminium cooking foil, shiny side upwards.

Place the moulds on two baking trays and bake in a moderately hot oven (190C, 375F, gas 5) for 20 minutes. Remove the baking beans and paper or the foil and cook for a further 10 minutes, or until lightly browned. Allow the biscuits to cool in the tins for a few minutes before transferring them to a wire rack to cool completely.

Meanwhile, break the chocolate cake covering into pieces and place in a bowl over a saucepan of hot water. Heat gently, stirring occasionally, until melted. Dip each boat in the chocolate cake covering and drain off any excess, then place the boats on non-stick baking parchment or waxed paper. When half set, decorate the boats with liquorice allsorts, or fix paper sails and fill the boats with sweets, as shown in the photograph on page 85.

Leave the chocolate boats to set completely before serving them. *Makes 24 chocolate boats*

Chocolate Chequerboards

175 g/6 oz butter or margarine, softened
175 g/6 oz caster sugar
1 egg, lightly beaten
350 g/12 oz plain flour, sifted
50 g/2 oz plain chocolate
15 g/$\frac{1}{2}$ oz cocoa

Lightly grease two baking trays. Cream the butter or margarine with the sugar until very soft, light and fluffy. Gradually add the egg, beating continuously. Divide the creamed mixture into two portions of approximately 250 g/9 oz and 150 g/5 oz. Work 100 g/4 oz of the flour into the smaller portion.

Break the chocolate into pieces and place in a bowl over a saucepan of hot water. Heat gently, stirring occasionally, until the chocolate has melted. Sift the cocoa and the remaining flour into a bowl, then work these dry ingredients into the larger portion of creamed mixture, together with the melted chocolate.

Divide the plain dough into six and roll each piece into a sausage shape, 35 cm/14 in long, on a lightly floured board. Divide the chocolate flavoured dough into approximately two thirds and one third. Divide the smaller portion into five and roll each piece into a sausage shape in the same manner as the plain dough. Place a plain and chocolate flavoured roll side by side, then arrange the remaining rolls on top of these, alternating the colours to form a chequerboard.

Roll the remaining chocolate flavoured dough into a rectangle measuring 35 × 15 cm/14 × 6 in. Wrap the dough carefully around the chequer rolls, placing the join on the underside. Wrap the roll in cling film or foil and chill overnight in the refrigerator.

To finish, cut the roll into 5-mm/$\frac{1}{4}$-in slices and place the slices at intervals on the prepared baking trays. Bake in a moderately hot oven (200 C, 400 F, gas 6) for 10–12 minutes, or until darkened in colour and cooked. Remove the hot biscuits from the trays and transfer them to a wire rack to cool completely. *Makes 40 chequerboards*

Chocolate Dominos

100 g/4 oz butter or margarine, softened
100 g/4 oz soft, light brown sugar
1 egg yolk
200 g/7 oz plain flour
25 g/1 oz cocoa powder
175 g/6 oz chocolate and hazelnut spread

Decoration
$\frac{1}{2}$ quantity Glacé Icing (page 125)

Lightly grease two baking trays and make a greaseproof paper piping bag, according to the instructions on page 126. Cream the butter or margarine with the sugar until very soft, light and fluffy, then beat in the egg yolk. Sift the flour and cocoa into a bowl, then gradually work these dry ingredients into the creamed mixture to make a fairly firm dough.

Knead the dough lightly, then wrap it in cling film and chill for 30 minutes, or longer if you have time. Roll out the dough on a lightly floured board to a rectangle measuring 20 × 30 cm/ 8 × 12 in. Using a long knife, cut the rectangle into smaller rectangles, measuring 2.5 × 5 cm/1 × 2 in. Using a palette knife, carefully transfer the biscuits to the prepared baking trays.

Bake in a moderate oven (180C, 350F, gas 4) for about 12 minutes, or until darkened in colour and cooked. Remove the hot biscuits from the trays and transfer them to a wire rack to cool completely.

Sandwich the biscuits together in pairs with the chocolate and hazelnut spread. To decorate the biscuits, make the glacé icing according to the recipe instructions and pour it into the paper piping bag. Cut a tiny hole in the point of the bag and pipe a line across half way down each biscuit, then pipe one to six dots at each end. *Makes 24 chocolate dominos*

Chocolate Monsters

100 g/4 oz butter or margarine, softened
75 g/3 oz soft, light brown sugar
25 g/1 oz soft, dark brown sugar
1 egg, lightly beaten
225 g/8 oz self-raising flour
25 g/1 oz cocoa powder

Filling and decoration
1 quantity Chocolate Butter Icing (page 124)
225 g/8 oz milk or plain chocolate flavoured cake covering
4 liquorice strands
32 smarties
$\frac{1}{2}$ quantity Glacé Icing (page 125)

Lightly grease two baking trays and make a greaseproof paper piping bag according to the instructions on page 126. Cream the butter or margarine with the sugars until very soft, light and fluffy. Gradually add the egg, beating continuously. Sift together the flour and cocoa, then work these dry ingredients into the creamed mixture.

Divide the mixture into 32, then form each piece into a ball. Place well apart on the prepared baking trays. Bake in a moderately hot oven (190 C, 375 F, gas 5) for 12–15 minutes, or until slightly darkened in colour and cooked. Remove the hot biscuits from the trays and transfer them to a wire rack to cool completely.

While the biscuits are cooling, make the chocolate butter icing and glacé icing according to the recipe instructions. To finish the monsters, sandwich the biscuits together in pairs with the butter icing. Break the cake covering into pieces and place in a basin over a saucepan of hot water. Heat gently, stirring occasionally, until melted. Place the sandwiched biscuits on a wire rack and stand the rack over a clean baking tray. Coat the biscuits with the chocolate cake covering.

Just before the chocolate sets, apply liquorice antennae and smartie eyes. Pour the glacé icing into the paper piping bag. Cut a tiny hole in the point of the bag and pipe a nose and a mouth on each biscuit to complete the monster's face. When completely set, transfer the monsters to paper cake cases before serving. *Makes 16 chocolate monsters*

Chocolate Brownies

100 g/4 oz plain chocolate
50 g/2 oz butter or margarine
175 g/6 oz soft, light brown sugar
2 eggs, lightly beaten
175 g/6 oz self-raising flour, sifted
50 g/2 oz walnuts, chopped

Lightly grease and line a 28 × 18-cm/11 × 7-in Swiss roll tin. Break the chocolate into pieces and place in a bowl over a saucepan of hot water. Add the butter or margarine and heat gently, stirring occasionally, until both chocolate and butter have melted.

Remove from the heat, cool slightly, then beat in the sugar and eggs. Mix together the flour and walnuts and fold these dry ingredients into the chocolate mixture. Pour the mixture into the prepared tin, tipping the tin slightly so that the mixture spreads into the corners.

Bake in a moderate oven (180 C, 350 F, gas 4) for 30 minutes, or until just firm to the touch. Cool the baked brownie in the tin for a few minutes before cutting it into squares and transferring the brownies to a wire rack to cool completely. *Makes 16 brownies*

Banana and Chocolate Chip Cookies

(Illustrated on page 85)

100 g/4 oz butter or margarine, softened
100 g/4 oz demerara sugar
1 egg, lightly beaten
½ teaspoon vanilla essence
100 g/4 oz banana chips
175 g/6 oz self-raising flour
50 g/2 oz chocolate chips

Lightly grease two baking trays. Cream the butter or margarine with the sugar until very soft, light and fluffy. Gradually add the egg, beating continuously, then beat in the vanilla essence.

Spread the banana chips between two pieces of greaseproof paper and crush them lightly with a rolling pin. Stir the banana chips into the creamed mixture, together with the flour and chocolate chips.

Drop heaped teaspoonfuls of the mixture, sufficiently apart to allow room for spreading, on to the prepared baking trays and flatten slightly with the back of a fork.

Bake in a moderate oven (170C, 325F, gas 3) for 15–20 minutes, or until golden. Leave the cookies to cool on the trays for a few minutes before transferring them to a wire rack to cool completely. *Makes 30 banana and chocolate chip cookies*

Variation

Chocolate and nut chip cookies: follow the method for banana and chocolate chip cookies, but replace the banana chips with 50 g/2 oz roughly chopped walnuts.

Opposite *Clockwise, from top left:* Lollipop Biscuits (page 95); Banana and Chocolate Chip Cookies (page 84); Chocolate Boats (page 78)

Peanut Butter Cookies

100 g/4 oz crunchy peanut butter
100 g/4 oz butter or margarine
100 g/4 oz caster sugar
75 g/3 oz soft, light brown sugar
2 eggs, lightly beaten
225 g/8 oz self-raising flour, sifted
20 peanuts, halved

Lightly grease two baking trays. Cream together the peanut butter, butter or margarine and sugars until very soft, light and fluffy. Gradually add the eggs, beating continuously, then work the flour into the creamed mixture to give a fairly soft dough.

Divide the dough into 40, then roll each piece into a ball the size of a walnut. Place the biscuits on the prepared baking trays, allowing room for them to spread. Flatten slightly with the prongs of a fork to produce a criss-cross pattern and press a peanut half in the centre of each biscuit.

Bake the peanut butter cookies in a moderate oven (180 C, 350 F, gas 4) for 20–25 minutes, or until golden brown. Using a palette knife, carefully remove the hot biscuits from the trays and transfer them to a wire rack to cool completely. *Makes 40 peanut butter cookies*

Opposite *From the top:* Walnut and Ginger Shortcakes (page 110); Langues de Chat (page 100); Chocolate Brandy Log (page 102); Almond Tuiles (page 99); Citrus Lace Cups (page 105)

Neapolitan Cookies

(Illustrated on front cover)

100 g/4 oz butter or margarine, softened
100 g/4 oz caster sugar
1 egg, lightly beaten
225 g/8 oz plain flour
1 teaspoon baking powder
1 sachet chocolate flavoured blancmange powder
1 sachet banana flavoured blancmange powder
1 sachet strawberry flavoured blancmange powder
a little red food colouring

Lightly grease two baking trays. Cream the butter or margarine with the sugar until very soft, light and fluffy. Gradually add the egg, beating continuously. Sift together the flour and baking powder, then work these dry ingredients into the creamed mixture.

Divide the mixture into three, then add a different blancmange flavour to each portion and mix well to make a soft dough. Add a drop of red food colouring to the strawberry flavoured dough if necessary. On a lightly floured board, roll each piece of dough into a long sausage shape 1-cm/½-in in diameter. Place the chocolate and banana flavoured rolls side by side, then lay the strawberry flavoured roll down the centre. Press lightly together, wrap in cling film or foil and chill the roll overnight in the refrigerator.

To finish the cookies, cut the roll into 5 mm/¼ in slices and place these at intervals on the prepared baking trays. Bake the biscuits in a moderately hot oven (200 C, 400 F, gas 6) for 10–12 minutes, or until darkened in colour and cooked.

Carefully remove the hot biscuits from the trays and transfer them to a wire rack to cool completely. *Makes 60 Neapolitan cookies*

Orange and Lemon Pinwheels

100 g/4 oz butter or margarine, softened
100 g/4 oz caster sugar
1 egg, lightly beaten
275 g/10 oz plain flour, sifted
grated rind of 1 orange
a few drops of orange food colouring
grated rind of 1 lemon
a few drops of yellow food colouring

Lightly grease two baking trays. Cream the butter or margarine with the sugar until very soft, light and fluffy. Gradually add the egg, beating continuously. Divide the creamed mixture in two.

Work half the flour, the orange rind and a few drops of orange colouring into one half of the creamed mixture and the remaining flour, the lemon rind and a few drops of yellow food colouring into the other half. Knead each piece of dough lightly and roll out on a floured board to a rectangle measuring 30 × 15 cm/12 × 6 in. Using a rolling pin to help you, carefully lay the sheet of lemon flavoured dough over the sheet of orange flavoured dough, then roll up lengthwise like a Swiss roll. Wrap the roll of dough in cling film or foil and chill it overnight in the refrigerator.

Cut the roll into 5-mm/$\frac{1}{4}$-in slices and place the slices at intervals on the prepared baking trays. Bake in a moderately hot oven (200 C, 400 F, gas 6) for 10–12 minutes, or until darkened in colour and cooked. Remove the hot biscuits from the trays and transfer them to a wire rack to cool completely.
Makes 30 orange and lemon pinwheels

Krispie Meringues

rice paper
150 g/5 oz icing sugar
2 egg whites
50 g/2 oz chopped, mixed nuts
25 g/1 oz Rice Krispies
6 glacé cherries

Line two baking trays with rice paper. Whisk the icing sugar and egg whites over hot water until stiff enough to form peaks. Remove the mixture from the heat and carefully fold in the nuts and cereal.

Place heaped tablespoonfuls of the mixture at intervals on the rice paper. Halve the glacé cherries and use them to decorate the meringues.

Bake the meringues in a cool oven (150 C, 300 F, gas 2) for 25 minutes, or until very slightly browned and crisp on the outside. Allow the meringues to cool on the trays for a few minutes, then tear the excess rice paper away and transfer the meringues to a wire rack to cool completely. *Makes 12 krispie meringues*

Millionaire's Shortbread

250 g/10 oz butter or margarine, softened
75 g/3 oz caster sugar
225 g/8 oz plain flour
25 g/1 oz rice flour
½ (400-g/14.1-oz) can condensed milk
2 tablespoons golden syrup
175 g/6 oz plain chocolate, grated

Lightly grease an 18 × 23-cm/7 × 9-in Swiss roll tin. Cream 175 g/6 oz of the butter or margarine with the sugar until very soft, light and fluffy. Sift together the flour and rice flour and gradually work these dry ingredients into the creamed mixture. Press the mixture into the prepared tin and smooth the surface with the back of a warm metal spoon. Chill for 1–2 hours.

Bake the shortbread in a moderate oven (180 C, 350 F, gas 4) for about 40 minutes, or until it is a pale straw colour. Leave in the tin to cool completely.

While the shortbread is cooling, make the topping. Melt the remaining fat, the condensed milk and syrup in a saucepan over a low heat. Bring to the boil and boil steadily for 5 minutes, stirring continuously. Pour the toffee over the cold biscuit base. While the toffee is still hot, sprinkle it evenly with chocolate and allow the chocolate to melt.

Cut the shortbread into squares when the topping is set, using a hot metal knife. *Makes 12 pieces of millionaire's shortbread*

Butterscotch Bars

4 eggs
350 g/12 oz soft, light brown sugar
225 g/8 oz plain flour, sifted
225 g/8 oz chopped mixed nuts

Line an 18 × 27-cm/7 × 11-in Swiss roll tin with non-stick baking parchment. Place the eggs and sugar in a large bowl standing over a saucepan of hot water. Whisk until the mixture is thick enough to leave a trail for at least 6 seconds.

Remove from the heat and whisk until cold. Re-sift the flour over the mixture and fold it in gently, using a metal spoon and a figure of eight motion. Finally, fold in the nuts. Pour the mixture evenly into the prepared tin and gently smooth the surface with the back of a warm metal spoon.

Bake in a moderate oven (180C, 350F, gas 4) for about 15 minutes, or until firm to the touch. Allow to cool completely before marking and cutting into fingers and serving. *Makes 24 butterscotch bars*

Milk Mice

$\frac{1}{2}$ quantity of biscuit dough for
Jammy Faces (page 96)

Decoration
2 tablespoons custard powder
2 tablespoons caster sugar
150 ml/$\frac{1}{4}$ pint milk, plus 2 tablespoons
2 egg yolks
25 g/1 oz butter
275 g/10 oz white chocolate, grated
50 g/2 oz malted milk biscuits, lightly crushed
3 liquorice strands
16 flaked almonds
16 silver balls

Make the dough according to the recipe instructions. Lightly grease a baking tray, draw and cut out a pear-shaped cardboard pattern 7.5 cm/3 in. in length and 5 cm/2 in at the widest part.

Roll out the biscuit dough on a lightly floured board to a thickness of 5 mm/¼ in. Using the cardboard pattern as a guide, cut out the dough with a knife, re-rolling the trimmings, if necessary, to make eight mice. Carefully transfer the biscuits to the prepared baking tray, using a palette knife. Chill for 30 minutes, or longer if you have time.

Bake the biscuits in a moderate oven (180C, 350F, gas 4) for 18–20 minutes, or until lightly browned. Remove the hot biscuits from the trays and transfer them to a wire rack to cool completely.

While the biscuits are cooling, make the topping. Blend the custard powder and sugar with enough milk from the 150 ml/¼ pint to make a smooth paste. Bring the remaining milk to the boil and quickly stir it into the custard mixture. Return the custard to the saucepan and cook for a couple of minutes over a low heat, stirring continuously, until very thick. Remove the custard from the heat and beat in the egg yolks, butter and 100 g/4 oz of the grated chocolate. Allow to cool completely, then stir in the crushed biscuits. Pile this mixture on top of the biscuit bases. Smooth the mixture with a wet palette knife, tapering off at the narrowest part to form a nose.

Place the remaining chocolate and the 2 tablespoons of milk in a basin over a saucepan of hot water. Heat gently, stirring occasionally, until the chocolate has melted. Place the mice shapes on a wire rack standing over a clean baking tray and coat them with the chocolate. Just before the chocolate sets, decorate the mice with liquorice for tails and whiskers, flaked almonds for ears and silver balls for eyes. Allow to set before serving the biscuits. *Makes 8 milk mice*

Gingerbread Men

450 g/1 lb plain flour
$\frac{1}{4}$ teaspoon salt
2 teaspoons bicarbonate of soda
2 teaspoons ground ginger
1 teaspoon ground cinnamon
100 g/4 oz butter or margarine
225 g/8 oz soft, light brown sugar
4 tablespoons golden syrup
1 egg, lightly beaten

Decoration
$\frac{1}{2}$ quantity Glacé Icing (page 125)

Lightly grease two baking trays and make a greaseproof paper piping bag according to the instructions on page 126. Sift the flour, salt, bicarbonate of soda, ginger and cinnamon into a bowl and make a well in the centre. Melt the butter or margarine, sugar and syrup in a saucepan over a low heat. Do not allow the mixture to boil. Cool slightly, then pour into the well in the dry ingredients. Add the egg and mix well to form a soft dough.

Knead the dough lightly, then roll it out on a floured board to a thickness of 5 mm/$\frac{1}{4}$ in. Cut the dough into shapes, using a special cutter, or draw a gingerbread man on cardboard, cut it out and use as a pattern. Using a palette knife, carefully transfer the gingerbread men to the prepared baking trays, spacing them a little apart to allow room for spreading.

Bake the biscuits in a moderate oven (170 C, 325 F, gas 3) for 20 minutes, or until darkened in colour and cooked. Carefully remove the hot biscuits from the trays and transfer them to a wire rack to cool completely.

While the biscuits are cooling, prepare the glacé icing according to the recipe instructions and pour it into the paper piping bag. Cut a tiny hole in the point of the bag and pipe clothes and facial features on the gingerbread men. *Makes about 20 gingerbread men, according to the size of the cutter*

Lollipop Biscuits

(Illustrated on page 85)

175 g/6 oz butter or margarine, softened
175 g/6 oz caster sugar · 1 egg, lightly beaten
350 g/12 oz plain flour · 2 tablespoons cornflour
10 flat lollipop sticks

Decoration
double quantity Glacé Icing (page 125)
or 1 quantity Royal Icing (page 126)
a selection of food colourings
20 smarties

Lightly grease two baking trays. Cream the butter or margarine with the sugar until very soft, light and fluffy. Gradually add the egg, beating continuously. Sift the flour with the cornflour, then work these dry ingredients into the creamed mixture to make a fairly firm dough.

Knead lightly, then roll out the dough on a lightly floured board to a thickness of 3 mm/$\frac{1}{8}$ in. Cut into 20 rounds, using a 6.5-cm/2$\frac{1}{2}$-in plain cutter. Carefully sandwich two rounds of biscuit dough with a lollipop stick in between. Using a palette knife, transfer the biscuits to the prepared baking trays and chill for 30 minutes.

Bake in a moderate oven (180 C, 350 F, gas 4) for 15 minutes, or until lightly browned. Remove the hot biscuits from the trays and transfer them to a wire rack to cool completely.

While the biscuits are cooling, make the glacé or royal icing, according to the recipe instructions, and four greaseproof paper piping bags (or more, depending on the number of colours you wish to decorate the lollipops with). Divide half the glacé icing into four portions, add a different food colouring to each portion and spoon into the paper piping bags.

Spread each of the cooled biscuits with white icing and apply smarties for eyes. Snip the ends off the paper piping bags and pipe in hair and features, as in the photograph on page 85. Allow the icing to set before serving the lollipops. *Makes 10 lollipop biscuits*

Jammy Faces

(Illustrated on front cover)

100 g/4 oz butter or margarine, softened
50 g/2 oz caster sugar
175 g/6 oz plain flour
225 g/8 oz seedless raspberry jam

Lightly grease two baking trays. Cream the butter or margarine with the sugar until very soft, light and fluffy. Sift the flour into a bowl, then work it into the creamed mixture to form a firm dough.

Knead lightly, then roll out the dough on a floured board to a thickness of 5 mm/¼ in. Cut the dough with a 7.5-cm/3-in plain round cutter, then, using a palette knife, carefully transfer the rounds to the prepared baking trays. Using a variety of small cutters, cut eyes, nose and mouth from half the quantity of biscuits. Chill for 30 minutes, or longer if you have time.

Bake the biscuits in a moderate oven (180 C, 350 F, gas 4) for 18–20 minutes, or until lightly browned. Remove the hot biscuits from the trays and transfer them to a wire rack to cool completely.

To finish the biscuits, sandwich plain rounds and faces together in pairs with the jam. *Makes 5 jammy faces*

Variation
Traffic lights: roll the biscuit dough to a rectangle measuring just over 15 × 30 cm/6 × 12 in. Trim the edges and cut the rectangle into biscuits measuring 2.5 × 7.5 cm/1 × 3 in. Cut three 1-cm/½-in holes from half the biscuits, then bake and cool the biscuits as for jammy faces.

Sandwich plain and holed rectangles together with raspberry, apricot and greengage jam under holes one, two and three respectively. *Makes 12 traffic lights*

The Three Bears

100 g/4 oz butter or margarine, softened
100 g/4 oz caster sugar
1 egg, lightly beaten
grated rind of 1 lemon
275 g/10 oz plain flour
2 teaspoons mixed spice
1 teaspoon cinnamon

Decoration
12 currants
glacé cherries
angelica
flaked almonds

Lightly grease two baking trays and cut out three cardboard bear shapes in graduating sizes. Cream the butter or margarine with the sugar until very soft, light and fluffy. Gradually add the egg, beating continuously, then beat in the lemon rind. Sift together the flour and spices, then work these dry ingredients into the creamed mixture to make a fairly firm dough. Knead lightly, then roll out the dough on a floured board to a thickness of 5 mm/$\frac{1}{4}$ in. Using the cardboard bear shapes as a guide, cut out the dough with a knife, re-rolling the trimmings, if necessary, to make two families of three bears. Then, using a palette knife, carefully transfer the bears to the prepared baking trays, spacing the biscuits a little apart to allow room for spreading. Decorate with currants for eyes, pieces of cherry for nose and mouth, almonds for buttons and sliced angelica for bow ties.

Bake the bears in a moderate oven (180 C, 350 F, gas 4) for 15–20 minutes, or until lightly browned. Allow the biscuits to cool on the trays for a few minutes before carefully transferring them to a wire rack to cool completely. *Makes 2 families of 3 bears*

Dessert Biscuits

Biscuits tend to be regarded as the poor relation when it comes to choosing between the cake trolley and the biscuit barrel. Fine for offering to a neighbour who has just popped in for coffee, but quickly set to one side on special occasions.

This chapter goes a long way towards improving the reputation of the biscuit! It gives recipes for a variety of biscuits to serve for dessert as well as with dessert. Try serving Citrus Lace Cups at the end of your next dinner party when you want to impress, or wickedly indulgent Chocolate Brandy Log. Walnut and Ginger Shortcakes are not only delicious to eat, but very quick and easy to prepare. If you are really short of time, serve Langues de Chat or Caramel Palmiers with a good quality bought icecream, and nobody will realise you cheated!

Almond Tuiles

(Illustrated on page 86)

50 g/2 oz butter or margarine
2 egg whites
100 g/4 oz caster sugar
50 g/2 oz plain flour, sifted
grated rind of 1 orange
50 g/2 oz flaked or nibbed almonds

Line two baking trays with non-stick baking parchment. Melt the fat over a low heat, then leave it to cool until lukewarm.

Meanwhile, whisk the egg whites until stiff, but not too dry and gradually whisk in the sugar. Using a metal spoon, fold in half the flour, then pour the butter around the edge of the mixture in the bowl. Gradually add and fold in the remaining flour, at the same time working in the butter, orange rind and almonds.

Drop teaspoonfuls of the mixture well apart on the prepared baking trays and spread out to give thin rounds of about 6 cm/ 2½ in in diameter. Bake the biscuits in a moderately hot oven (190 C, 375 F, gas 5) for about 10 minutes, or until golden brown round the edges.

Using a large palette knife, carefully remove the biscuits from the trays while they are still hot. (If the mixture hardens on the trays, replace them in the oven for about half a minute until the biscuits soften.) Quickly wrap each almond tuile around an oiled rolling pin and place on a wire rack until cool.
Makes 35 almond tuiles

Variation
Cigarettes Russes: prepare and cook as almond tuiles, but omit the almonds and orange rind, then, instead of wrapping around a rolling pin, wrap the biscuits quickly around oiled wooden spoon handles.

Langues de Chat

(Illustrated on page 86)

50 g/2 oz butter or margarine, softened
50 g/2 oz caster sugar
40 g/1½ oz plain flour
2 egg whites

Line two baking trays with non-stick baking parchment. Cream the butter or margarine with the caster sugar until very soft, light and fluffy. Sift the flour and fold it into the creamed mixture. Whisk the egg whites until stiff, but not too dry and gently fold them into the mixture – the resulting paste should be just stiff enough to pipe.

Spoon the mixture into a large piping bag fitted with a 5-mm/¼-in plain nozzle. Pipe 7.5-cm/3-in strips of the mixture on to the prepared baking trays, spacing them a little apart to allow room for the biscuits to spread.

Bake in a moderately hot oven (200 C, 400 F, gas 6) for about 8 minutes, or until the edges of each biscuit are light golden. Allow the biscuits to cool on the trays for a few seconds, then transfer them to a wire rack to cool completely. *Makes 25 langues de chat*

Honey and Cinnamon Wafers

50 g/2 oz butter or margarine, softened
50 g/2 oz soft, light brown sugar
175 g/6 oz clear honey
1 egg, lightly beaten
50 g/2 oz plain flour
½ teaspoon ground cinnamon
50 g/2 oz shredded almonds

Line two baking trays with non-stick baking parchment. Cream the butter or margarine and sugar until very soft, light and fluffy. Stir in the honey, then gradually add the egg, beating continuously. Sift together the flour and cinnamon, then fold these dry ingredients into the creamed mixture. Finally fold in the almonds.

Drop teaspoonfuls of the mixture well apart on to the prepared baking trays and spread out to give thin, even rounds, about 5 cm/2 in in diameter.

Bake in a moderately hot oven (190C, 375F, gas 5) for about 10 minutes, or until golden brown. Allow the biscuits to cool on the trays for a few seconds, then, using a large palette knife, carefully transfer the biscuits to a wire rack to cool completely. *Makes 36 honey and cinnamon wafers*

Caramel Palmiers

100 g/4 oz caster sugar
1 (200-g/7-oz) packet frozen puff pastry, thawed

Lightly grease two baking trays. Sprinkle half the sugar in a fairly thick layer over the work surface. Roll the pastry out on this into a 25-cm/10-in square. Sprinkle the pastry thickly with the remaining sugar. Trim the edges if necessary, then roll the two longer sides to the centre to form a double roll. Cut the roll into 1-cm/½-in slices and press the cut sides into any sugar remaining on the table. Carefully transfer the slices to the prepared baking trays, spacing a little apart to allow room for them to spread.

Bake the biscuits in a hot oven (230C, 450F, gas 8) for 10–12 minutes, or until well risen and golden brown. Using a palette knife, remove the hot biscuits from the trays and transfer them to a wire rack to cool completely. *Makes 20 caramel palmiers*

Chocolate Brandy Log

(Illustrated on page 86)

175 g/6 oz butter or margarine
50 g/2 oz caster sugar
50 g/2 oz soft, light brown sugar
175 g/6 oz plain flour
25 g/1 oz cocoa

Filling and decoration
450 ml/¾ pint double cream
3 tablespoons brandy
2 tablespoons grated chocolate to decorate

Lightly grease two baking trays. Cream the butter or margarine with the sugars until very soft, light and fluffy. Sift together the flour and cocoa, then work these dry ingredients into the creamed mixture.

Divide the mixture into 15 and form each piece into a ball. Place at intervals on the prepared baking trays. Flatten slightly with a fork or knife dipped in cold water.

Bake in a moderate oven (180C, 350F, gas 4) for about 15 minutes, or until darkened in colour and cooked. Remove the hot biscuits from the trays and transfer them to a wire rack to cool completely.

To finish the log, whip the cream with the brandy until stiff. Sandwich the biscuits together with just under half the cream and brandy mixture to form a long roll. (This is best carried out on the serving plate.) Cover the roll with the remaining cream and brandy mixture, as shown in the photograph on page 86, and decorate with the grated chocolate. Chill for 1 hour before serving. *Makes 1 chocolate brandy log which serves 8*

Opposite *Clockwise, from top right:* Bacon Twists (page 115); Digestive Biscuits (page 112); Walnut Wheatmeal Crackers (page 112); Oatcakes (page 120); Cheese Nibbles (page 117)

Citrus Lace Cups

(Illustrated on page 86)

50 g/2 oz butter or margarine
50 g/2 oz caster sugar
50 g/2 oz golden syrup
grated rind of 2 oranges
50 g/2 oz plain flour, sifted
1 litre/1¾ pints lemon sorbet
pared rind of 1 lemon to decorate

Line two baking trays with non-stick baking parchment. Melt the fat, sugar and syrup in a saucepan over a low heat. Do not allow to boil. Stir in the orange rind, then cool the mixture slightly. Quickly fold in the flour.

Drop tablespoonfuls of the mixture well apart on the prepared baking trays. Bake the biscuits in a moderate oven (180C, 350F, gas 4) for about 10 minutes, or until thinly spread and golden.

Allow the biscuits to cool on the trays for a few seconds, then, using a large palette knife, carefully remove the biscuits from the trays while they are still hot. Quickly lay each biscuit over the top of an oiled wine glass to form the base of the basket, then mould the edges outwards to form the frilly basket shape shown in the photograph on page 86. Transfer the baskets to a wire rack and allow the biscuits to cool completely before filling them with sorbet. Sprinkle the lemon rind over the sorbet. *Makes 12 citrus lace cups*

Opposite Biscuit decoration

Strawberry Trumpets

(Illustrated on front cover)

50 g/2 oz butter
2 egg whites
100 g/4 oz caster sugar
50 g/2 oz plain flour, sifted
grated rind of 1 orange
300 ml/½ pint double cream
2 tablespoons orange liqueur
(for example Grand Marnier)

Decoration
225 g/8 oz strawberries

Line two baking trays with non-stick baking parchment. Melt the butter over a low heat, then leave to cool until lukewarm.

Meanwhile, whisk the egg whites until stiff but not too dry and gradually whisk in the sugar. Using a metal spoon, fold in half the flour, then pour the butter around the edge of the mixture in the bowl. Gradually add and fold in the remaining flour, at the same time working in the butter. Lastly fold in the orange rind.

Drop teaspoonfuls of the mixture well apart on the prepared baking trays and spread out to give thin, even rounds about 10 cm/4 in. in diameter. Bake in a moderately hot oven (190 C, 375 F, gas 5) for 7–8 minutes or until golden brown round the edges. Allow the biscuits to cool on the trays for a few seconds so that the mixture will stay together when lifted. Using a large palette knife, carefully remove the biscuits from the trays while they are still hot. (If the mixture hardens on the trays replace them in the oven for about half a minute, or until the biscuits soften.) Quickly wrap each biscuit around a cream horn tin and place on a wire rack until cool. Continue cooking the biscuits in this way until the mixture is used, re-lining the trays if necessary.

To finish the trumpets, whip the cream with the orange liqueur until stiff. Spoon the cream into a piping bag fitted with a star nozzle and pipe it into the trumpet shells. Decorate each one with a whole strawberry and serve within an hour of filling, or the biscuits will loose their crisp texture. *Makes about 15 strawberry trumpets*

Sultana Drops

75 g/3 oz sultanas
2 tablespoons brandy
2 eggs, plus 1 egg yolk
175 g/6 oz caster sugar
150 g/5 oz plain flour
2 tablespoons single cream

Line two baking trays with non-stick baking parchment. Place the sultanas and brandy in a small saucepan and heat gently until the fruit becomes plump and the brandy has been absorbed. Leave on one side to cool.

Put the eggs, egg yolk and sugar in a basin over a saucepan of hot water. Whisk until thick enough to leave a trail for 2–3 seconds, remove from the heat and whisk until cold. Sift the flour once into a bowl, then sift it lightly over the surface of the egg mixture. Fold the flour in gently with a large metal spoon. Finally fold in the cream.

Drop heaped teaspoonfuls of the mixture well apart on the prepared baking trays and sprinkle each one with a few sultanas. Bake the sultana drops in a moderately hot oven (190C, 375F, gas 5) for about 12 minutes, or until golden brown. Allow the biscuits to cool on the trays for a minute before transferring them to a wire rack to cool completely. *Makes 30 sultana drops*

Flakemeal Shortbread

100 g/4 oz butter or margarine, softened
50 g/2 oz demerara sugar
60 g/2½ oz plain flour
¼ teaspoon salt
¼ teaspoon bicarbonate of soda
100 g/4 oz rolled oats

Lightly grease a 23 × 15-cm/9 × 6-in shallow tin. Cream the butter or margarine with the sugar until very soft, light and fluffy. Sift together the flour, salt and bicarbonate of soda, then gradually work these dry ingredients into the creamed mixture, together with the rolled oats, to make a crumbly dough.

Press the dough into the prepared tin and smooth the surface with the back of a warm metal spoon. Prick all over with a fork, then chill for 1–2 hours.

Bake the shortbread in a moderate oven (180 C, 350 F, gas 4) for about 30 minutes, or until it is lightly browned. Cut the shortbread into 16 fingers while still hot, then leave to cool in the tin for a few minutes before transferring the fingers to a wire rack to cool completely. *Makes 16 flakemeal shortbread fingers*

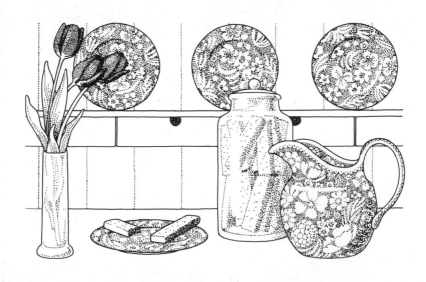

Strawberry Shortcake

175 g/6 oz butter or margarine, softened
50 g/2 oz icing sugar
225 g/8 oz plain flour, sifted
caster sugar to sprinkle

Filling and decoration
300 ml/$\frac{1}{2}$ pint double cream
2 tablespoons brandy
2 tablespoons icing sugar
450 g/1 lb strawberries

Lightly grease two baking trays. Cream the butter or margarine with the 50 g/2 oz icing sugar until very soft, light and fluffy. Gradually work the sifted flour into the creamed mixture to form a soft dough.

Knead the dough lightly, then wrap it in cling film and chill for 30 minutes, or longer if you have time. Divide the dough in half and roll out each piece on a lightly floured board to a 23-cm/9-in circle. Using a large palette knife, carefully transfer the rounds to the prepared baking trays.

Bake the shortcakes in a moderately hot oven (190 C, 375 F, gas 5) for about 15 minutes, or until lightly browned. Immediately they are removed from the oven, sprinkle the shortcakes with caster sugar. Allow them to cool completely on the trays.

Meanwhile, whip the cream with the brandy and the 2 tablespoons of icing sugar until thick. Wash, hull and slice all but three of the best strawberries and fold the slices into the cream mixture. Place one circle of shortbread on a flat serving plate and pile the strawberry and cream mixture on top. Mark and cut the second portion of shortbread into 10 sections. Reform the sections into a circle, pressing each one into the cream mixture at an angle of 45 degrees. Decorate the shortcake with the reserved strawberries. *Makes 10 pieces of strawberry shortcake*

Walnut and Ginger Shortcakes

(Illustrated on page 86)

175 g/6 oz butter or margarine, softened
75 g/3 oz caster sugar
250 g/9 oz plain flour, sifted
50 g/2 oz walnuts, roughly chopped

Filling and decoration
300 ml/$\frac{1}{2}$ pint double cream
50 g/2 oz stem ginger, in syrup
6 walnut halves

Lightly grease two baking trays. Cream the butter or margarine with the sugar until very soft, light and fluffy. Gradually work the sifted flour into the creamed mixture, together with the walnuts, to make a fairly firm dough. Knead lightly, then wrap the dough in cling film and chill for 30 minutes, or longer if you have time.

Roll out the dough on a lightly floured board to a thickness of 5 mm/$\frac{1}{4}$ in. Cut it into 12 rounds, using a plain 7-cm/$2\frac{3}{4}$-in cutter for the first six, and a 6-cm/$2\frac{1}{4}$-in plain cutter for the remaining six. Using a palette knife, carefully transfer the biscuits to the prepared baking trays.

Bake in a moderate oven (180 C, 350 F, gas 4) for about 30 minutes, or until the shortcakes are a pale straw colour. Leave the shortcakes to cool on the trays for a few minutes before transferring them to a wire rack to cool completely.

To finish the shortcakes, whip the cream with 4 tablespoons of the ginger syrup. Spoon 6 tablespoons of the mixture into a piping bag fitted with a large star nozzle and set aside. Roughly chop the stem ginger and fold it into the remaining cream and syrup mixture.

Sandwich one large and one small shortcake together with the chopped ginger cream. Pipe a rosette of cream on top of each shortcake sandwich and decorate with a halved walnut.
Makes 6 walnut and ginger shortcakes

Savoury and Semi-Sweet Biscuits

Extend your biscuit-making talents by trying a few of the
following savoury recipes. They make a delicious change
from the dull, dry commercial cream cracker. Walnut
Wheatmeal Crackers, Oatcakes and Digestive Biscuits
served with cheese, provide a savoury end to dinner parties.
Thickly spread with butter and topped with a variety of
cheeses, they can form the basis of a speedy lunch. Or for
something more warming and substantial on a cold winter's
day, serve Bacon Twists or Cheese Straws straight from the
oven with a bowl of home-made soup at lunch or supper time.
Many of the recipes make tempting nibbles to serve with
drinks and are just that little bit different from peanuts
and crisps.
You may well discover that savoury biscuits are more
popular than the sweet varieties, but remember to store
sweet and savoury biscuits separately to avoid
contamination of flavours.

Digestive Biscuits

(Illustrated on page 103)

225 g/8 oz wholemeal flour
50 g/2 oz medium oatmeal
1 teaspoon salt
50 g/2 oz margarine
50 g/2 oz lard
50 g/2 oz light, soft brown sugar
½ beaten egg

Lightly grease two baking trays. Mix together the flour, oatmeal and salt. Rub the margarine and lard into the flour until the mixture resembles fine breadcrumbs. Stir in the sugar, add the beaten egg and mix well to make a fairly firm dough.

Knead the dough lightly, then roll it out on a floured board to a thickness of 3 mm/⅛ in. Cut the dough into rounds using a 6-cm/2½-in plain cutter and, using a palette knife, carefully transfer the rounds to the prepared baking trays.

Bake the biscuits in a moderate oven (180 C, 350 F, gas 4) for about 25 minutes or until darkened in colour and cooked. Remove the hot biscuits from the trays and transfer them to a wire rack to cool completely. *Makes 20 digestive biscuits*

Walnut Wheatmeal Crackers

(Illustrated on page 103)

75 g/3 oz butter or margarine
225 g/8 oz wheatmeal flour
75 g/3 oz ground walnuts
1 egg, lightly beaten
2 tablespoons water
1 tablespoon sea salt

Lightly grease two baking trays. Rub the butter or margarine into the flour until the mixture resembles fine breadcrumbs. Stir in the ground walnuts, then bind the mixture to a fairly firm dough with the egg and water.

Knead lightly, then roll out the dough on a floured board into a rectangle measuring about 26 × 32 cm/10 × 12½ in. Trim the edges, then cut the rectangle into 6-cm/2½-in squares. Prick each biscuit evenly with a fork, brush with water and sprinkle with the salt.

Bake the walnut wheatmeal crackers in a moderately hot oven (190C, 375F, gas 5) for about 15–20 minutes, or until lightly browned. Remove the hot biscuits from the trays and transfer them to a wire rack to cool completely. *Makes 20 walnut wheatmeal crackers*

Water Biscuits

225 g/8 oz plain flour
1½ teaspoons baking powder
½ teaspoon salt
75 g/3 oz lard
2–3 tablespoons water

Lightly grease two baking trays. Sift the flour, baking powder and salt into a bowl. Rub in the lard until the mixture resembles fine breadcrumbs, then add the water and mix well to make a soft pliable dough.

Knead the dough lightly and roll it out very thinly on a floured board. Cut the dough into rounds, using a 7.5-cm/3-in plain cutter. Prick the biscuits all over with a fork and, using a palette knife, carefully transfer them to the prepared baking trays.

Bake the water biscuits in a hot oven (225C, 425F, gas 7) for about 8 minutes, or until puffy and golden brown. Remove the hot biscuits from the trays and transfer them to a wire rack to cool completely. *Makes 16 water biscuits*

Breadsticks

2 teaspoons dried yeast
1 teaspoon caster sugar
300 ml/$\frac{1}{2}$ pint lukewarm water
450 g/1 lb strong plain flour
2 teaspoons salt
1 egg, lightly beaten

Lightly grease three baking trays. Sprinkle the yeast and sugar over 150 ml/$\frac{1}{4}$ pint of the water. Whisk well and leave in a warm place for 10–15 minutes, or until frothy.

Sift the flour and salt into a bowl. Make a well in the centre and add the yeast mixture and the remaining water. Bind the mixture to a firm dough and knead it on a lightly floured board for 10 minutes, or until smooth. Rinse, dry and lightly grease the mixing bowl. Put in the dough, cover the bowl with oiled cling film and leave the dough to prove in a warm place for 30 minutes.

Turn out the dough on to a floured board and knead it lightly. Divide the dough into 36 and roll each piece into a pencil-thin stick, 20 cm/8 in in length. Place the sticks on the prepared baking trays, spacing a little apart to allow room for them to spread. Cover with oiled cling film and leave them to rise for 20 minutes. Glaze with the beaten egg.

Bake the breadsticks in a moderately hot oven (200 C, 400 F, gas 6) for 10 minutes, then reduce the temperature to moderate (180 C, 350 F, gas 4) for a further 20 minutes. Remove the hot breadsticks from the tray and either transfer them to a wire rack to cool completely, or serve them warm. *Makes 36 breadsticks*

Bacon Twists

(Illustrated on page 103)

1 (350-g/12.3-oz) packet frozen puff pastry, thawed
8 rashers rindless streaky bacon
1 egg, lightly beaten
2 tablespoons freshly grated Parmesan cheese

Lightly grease two baking trays. Roll out the thawed puff pastry on a lightly floured board into a rectangle measuring 23 × 50 cm/9 × 20 in. Cut the pastry in half to give two rectangles of 23 × 25 cm/9 × 10 in.

Lay the bacon edge to edge down the length of one sheet of pastry, then, using a rolling pin to help you, lay the second sheet of pastry over the top. Press the two rectangles firmly together and cut the pastry and bacon sandwich into 1.5-cm/¾-in strips with a sharp knife. Twist each strip loosely and place the strips slightly apart on the prepared baking trays. Glaze each one with the egg and sprinkle lightly with Parmesan.

Bake the bacon twists in a hot oven (230C, 450F, gas 8) for about 10–12 minutes, or until well risen and golden brown. Remove the hot twists from the trays and either transfer them to a wire rack to cool completely, or serve them warm. *Makes 16 bacon twists*

Variation
Anchovy twists: blend together 100 g/4 oz cream cheese and 2 tablespoons anchovy paste. Make the twists in the same manner as bacon twists, but replace the bacon with the cheese mixture.

After glazing the anchovy twists with beaten egg, sprinkle them lightly with paprika instead of Parmesan.

Cheese Straws

100 g/4 oz plain flour
¼ teaspoon salt
pinch of cayenne
50 g/2 oz butter or margarine
25 g/1 oz Parmesan cheese, finely grated
1 egg yolk
2 tablespoons cold water

Lightly grease two baking trays. Sift together the flour, salt and cayenne. Rub in the butter or margarine until the mixture resembles fine breadcrumbs, then stir in the Parmesan. Bind the mixture to a firm dough with the egg yolk and water.

Knead the dough lightly, then roll it out on a floured board to a rectangle 10 cm/4 in in width. Trim the edges and cut into 5-mm/¼-in strips along the width of the rectangle. Re-roll the trimmings and cut out a few rings with 5-cm/2-in and 3-cm/1¼-in plain cutters. Using a palette knife, carefully transfer the strips and rings to the prepared baking trays.

Bake the cheese straws in a moderately hot oven (200 C, 400 F, gas 6) for 10–15 minutes, or until they are a pale golden brown. Remove the hot biscuits from the trays and transfer them to a wire rack to cool completely. Put bundles of cheese straws into the cooked rings. *Makes about 5 bundles of cheese straws*

Variation
Cheese canapés: roll out the dough to a thickness of 3 mm/⅛ in. Cut it into rounds with a 3.5-cm/1½-in cutter. Bake and cool the biscuits in the same way as cheese straws.

Soften 225 g/8 oz of cream cheese and put it into a piping bag fitted with a large star nozzle. Pipe a swirl of cream cheese on to each biscuit and garnish with either a small piece of stuffed olive or gherkin, pineapple or a few snipped chives.

Cheese Nibbles

(Illustrated on page 103)

175 g/6 oz self-raising flour
$\frac{1}{4}$ teaspoon salt
50 g/2 oz ground almonds
100 g/4 oz butter or margarine
100 g/4 oz Gruyère cheese, finely grated
1 egg, lightly beaten, plus 1 egg yolk
1 tablespoon water
sesame seeds, poppy seeds, caraway seeds,
mustard seeds

Lightly grease two baking trays. Sift together the flour and salt, then stir in the ground almonds. Rub in the butter or margarine until the mixture resembles fine breadcrumbs. Stir in the cheese, then add the beaten egg and mix well to make a pliable dough.

Knead lightly, then wrap the dough in cling film and chill it for 30 minutes, or longer if you have time. Roll the dough out on a lightly floured board to a thickness of 3 mm/$\frac{1}{8}$ in. Cut it into shapes, using a selection of small cocktail cutters. Carefully transfer the shapes to the prepared baking trays. Beat the egg yolk with the water and lightly brush the glaze over the biscuits, then sprinkle them thickly with seeds.

Bake the cheese nibbles in a moderate oven (180 C, 350 F, gas 4) for about 15 minutes, or until lightly browned. Remove the hot biscuits from the trays and transfer them to a wire rack to cool completely. Continue cooking batches of biscuits in this way until all the mixture is used, cleaning and re-greasing the trays if necessary. *Makes about 180 cheese nibbles*

Cheese Sablés

100 g/4 oz butter
100 g/4 oz plain flour
¼ teaspoon mustard powder
¼ teaspoon salt
100 g/4 oz Cheddar cheese, finely grated
1 egg, lightly beaten

Lightly grease two baking trays. Cream the butter until very soft, light and fluffy. Sift the flour with the mustard powder and salt, then stir these dry ingredients into the creamed butter, together with the cheese, and work all the ingredients together to form a firm dough.

Knead lightly, then wrap the dough in cling film and chill for 1 to 2 hours. Roll the dough out on a lightly floured board into a 23-cm/9-in square. Divide the square into 3.5-cm/1½-in squares, then cut these in half diagonally to give bite-sized triangles. Using a palette knife, carefully transfer the triangles to the prepared baking trays and brush them with the beaten egg. Chill any remaining biscuits and cook them as a second batch.

Bake the biscuits in a moderately hot oven (190C, 375F, gas 5) for 10–12 minutes, or until golden brown. Remove the hot biscuits from the trays and transfer them to a wire rack to cool completely. *Makes 128 cheese sablés*

Marmite and Cheese Palmiers

1 (350-g/12.3-oz) packet frozen puff pastry, thawed
2 tablespoons marmite
1 tablespoon milk
100 g/4 oz Cheshire cheese, finely grated
50 g/2 oz onion, finely grated

Lightly grease two baking trays. Roll out the puff pastry on a lightly floured board to a rectangle measuring 46 × 30 cm/ 18 × 12 in. Trim the edges if necessary.

Blend together the marmite and milk and brush the solution evenly over the surface of the pastry, then sprinkle the cheese and onion over the top. Roll the two longer sides to the centre to form a double roll, then cut into 1-cm/½-in slices. Using a palette knife, carefully transfer the palmiers to the prepared baking trays, spacing them a little apart to allow room for them to spread.

Bake the biscuits in a hot oven (230C, 450F, gas 8) for 10–12 minutes, or until they are well risen and golden brown. Remove the hot biscuits from the trays and either transfer them to a wire rack to cool completely, or serve them warm. *Makes about 45 marmite and cheese palmiers*

Variation
Mustard and cheese palmiers: replace the marmite and milk with 2 tablespoons of wholegrain mustard.

Oatcakes

(Illustrated on page 103)

100 g/4 oz wholewheat flour
1 level teaspoon salt
2 level teaspoons baking powder
225 g/8 oz medium oatmeal
50 g/2 oz lard or dripping
6 tablespoons hot water

Lightly grease two baking trays. Sift together the flour, salt and baking powder, then stir in the oatmeal. Rub in the lard or dripping until the mixture resembles fine breadcrumbs. Bind the mixture to a firm but pliable dough with the water.

Knead the dough lightly, then roll it out on a floured board to a thickness of 3 mm/⅛ in. Cut the dough into rounds using a 7.5-cm/3-in plain cutter and, using a palette knife, carefully transfer these to the prepared baking trays.

Bake the oatcakes in a cool oven (150 C, 300 F, gas 2) for about 25 minutes, or until cooked. Remove the hot biscuits from the trays and transfer them to a wire rack to cool completely. *Makes 16 oatcakes*

Herby Onion Wedges

350 g/12 oz plain flour
½ teaspoon salt
150 g/5 oz butter or margarine
50 g/2 oz onion, finely chopped
1 clove garlic, crushed
2 teaspoons mixed herbs
8 tablespoons cold water
2 tablespoons freshly grated Parmesan cheese

Lightly grease three baking trays. Sift the flour and salt into a bowl and rub in the butter or margarine until the mixture resembles fine breadcrumbs. Stir in the onion, garlic and herbs and bind the mixture to a fairly firm dough with the water.

Knead the dough lightly, then divide it into three pieces. Roll out each piece of dough on a floured board into a circle 23 cm/ 8 in. in diameter. Using two large palette knives, carefully transfer to the prepared baking trays, then cut each circle into eight wedges and sprinkle them lightly with Parmesan.

Bake the herby onion wedges in a moderately hot oven (200C, 400F, gas 6) for 25 minutes, or until lightly browned. Remove the hot biscuits from the trays and transfer them to a wire rack to cool completely. *Makes 32 herby onion wedges*

Savoury Onion Pretzels

175 g/6 oz butter or margarine
225 g/8 oz plain flour
packet dried onion soup mix
1 teaspoon celery seeds
2 eggs, lightly beaten

Lightly grease two baking trays. Cream the butter or margarine until very soft, light and fluffy. Mix the flour with the onion soup and celery seeds, then work half the dry mixture into the creamed fat. Gradually add the eggs, beating continuously, adding a tablespoon of flour if the mixture shows signs of curdling. Finally work in the remaining flour mixture to give a fairly firm dough.

Divide the dough into 24, then form each piece into a long, pencil-thin roll and shape it into a pretzel on the prepared baking trays. Loop the strip of dough into a loosely knotted circle, leaving fairly long ends. Press the ends neatly on the dough at the base of the circle.

Bake the pretzels in a moderate oven (180C, 350F, gas 4) for about 10–15 minutes, or until they are lightly browned. Remove the hot biscuits from the trays and transfer them to a wire rack to cool completely. *Makes 24 savoury onion pretzels*

Arrowroot Biscuits

100 g/4 oz plain flour
100 g/4 oz arrowroot
50 g/2 oz butter or margarine
100 g/4 oz caster sugar
1 egg, lightly beaten

Lightly grease two baking trays. Sift together the flour and arrowroot. Rub in the butter or margarine until the mixture resembles fine breadcrumbs, then stir in the sugar. Add the beaten egg and mix well to make a stiff dough.

Knead the dough lightly and roll it out on a floured board to a thickness of 3 mm/⅛ in. Cut the dough into rounds using a 6-cm/2½-in plain cutter. Prick the rounds all over with a fork then, using a palette knife, carefully transfer them to the prepared baking trays.

Bake the arrowroot biscuits in a moderate oven (180 C, 350 F, gas 4) for about 18–20 minutes, or until lightly browned. Remove the hot biscuits from the trays and transfer them to a wire rack to cool completely. *Makes 24 arrowroot biscuits*

Spicy Peanut Bars

225 g/8 oz plain flour
pinch of salt
¼ teaspoon black pepper
1 teaspoon cayenne
175 g/6 oz butter or margarine
100 g/4 oz Cheddar cheese, finely grated
100 g/4 oz salted peanuts, roughly chopped

Grease a 15 × 23-cm/6 × 9-in shallow tin. Sift the flour, salt, black pepper and ½ teaspoon of the cayenne into a bowl. Rub in the butter or margarine until the mixture resembles fine breadcrumbs. Stir in the grated cheese, then knead well to make a firm dough.

Knead lightly, then press the dough evenly into the prepared tin. Cover with an even layer of the peanuts and press them well into the mixture with the back of a metal spoon. Sprinkle the remaining cayenne over the nuts. Bake the mixture in a moderate oven (180C, 350F, gas 4) for 25–30 minutes.

Cut the hot mixture into fingers and leave in the tin for a few minutes before transferring the fingers to a wire rack to cool completely. *Makes 16 spicy peanut bars*

Potato Crackers

175 g/6 oz plain flour
1 teaspoon salt
50 g/2 oz butter or margarine
50 g/2 oz lard
100 g/4 oz mashed potato
1 egg, lightly beaten

Lightly grease two baking trays. Sift the flour and salt into a bowl, then rub in the butter or margarine and lard until the mixture resembles fine breadcrumbs. Work in the mashed potato to give a firm dough.

Knead the dough lightly, then wrap it in cling film and chill for 30 minutes, or longer if you have time. Roll the dough out on a lightly floured board into a 20-cm/8-in square, then cut the sheet of dough into 16 5-cm/2-in squares. Using a palette knife, carefully transfer the squares to the prepared baking trays and glaze them with the beaten egg.

Bake the potato crackers in a moderately hot oven (190C, 375F, gas 5) for about 20 minutes, or until golden brown. Remove the hot biscuits from the trays and transfer them to a wire rack to cool completely. *Makes 16 potato crackers*

Fillings and Icings

Butter Icing

100 g/4 oz butter, softened
175 g/6 oz icing sugar

Cream the butter until light and fluffy. Sift the icing sugar into a bowl and beat half the quantity at a time into the creamed butter. Flavour and colour as required.

Variations
Chocolate: melt 50 g/2 oz of plain or milk chocolate in a basin over a saucepan of hot water and add it to the butter icing, together with a few drops of vanilla essence.
Coffee: add 2 teaspoons of coffee essence, or 2 teaspoons of instant coffee granules dissolved in 1 teaspoon hot water, to the butter icing.

Fudge Icing

40 g/1½ oz butter
75 g/3 oz soft, light brown sugar
3 tablespoons milk
75 g/3 oz icing sugar, sifted

Melt the butter over a gentle heat. Add the brown sugar and milk and stir gently until the sugar has dissolved. Bring to the boil and boil for 1 minute. Cool the mixture slightly, then beat in the icing sugar. Flavour as required. Use the fudge icing quickly before it becomes too hard to handle.

Variation
Ginger: sift 1 teaspoon of ground ginger with the icing sugar before adding to the melted mixture.

Glacé Icing

225 g/8 oz icing sugar
about 2 tablespoons hot water

Sift the icing sugar into a bowl and add sufficient water to make a thick icing. Flavour and colour as required.

Variations
Orange or lemon: substitute freshly squeezed orange or lemon juice for the water.
Coffee: blend 1 tablespoon of instant coffee granules with the water before making up the icing.

Royal Icing

450 g / 1 lb icing sugar · 2 egg whites
1 teaspoon lemon juice

Sift the icing sugar twice. Place the egg whites in a bowl and whisk very lightly. Add half the icing sugar and the lemon juice and stir until mixed.

Gradually beat in the remaining icing sugar until the required consistency is obtained. If possible, leave the icing overnight before use. Flavour and colour as required.

TO MAKE A PIPING BAG

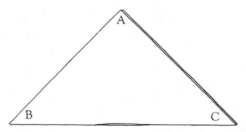

Fold a 25-cm / 10-in square of greaseproof paper in half to form a triangle. Make a small slit in the centre of the folded line to help give a sharp tip.

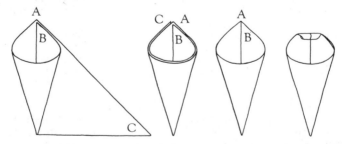

Roll corner B to the inside of corner A, then fold corner C round the outside of the bag to lie behind A. After making sure that all corners meet exactly and the bottom of the bag is closed in a sharp point, fold A over twice to keep the bag intact.

Index

Index